CELIAC DISEASE COOKBOOK FOR BEGINNERS

1200 Days of Wholesome Delights | Embark on
a Flavorful Journey to Nourish Your Body and
Embrace a Gluten-Free Lifestyle with Confidence

LANE NELSON

TABLE OF CONTENTS

INTRODUCTION

As gluten is found in many of the foods we consume daily, individuals diagnosed with celiac disease are compelled to drastically change their diets – often facing a bewildering array of new restrictions and limited food choices.

This cookbook is your essential guide that bridges the gap between health requirements and culinary satisfaction for people with celiac disease. It is designed to help you embrace a gluten-free lifestyle without sacrificing taste or convenience. It offers an extensive collection of mouthwatering gluten-free recipes that cater to diverse palates, dietary needs, and culinary skill levels.

Within these pages, you will explore a world of delightful dishes for every meal of the day – from appetizing breakfasts and tantalizing entrées to decadent desserts and scrumptious snacks. Each recipe has been meticulously crafted and extensively tested by experts in gluten-free cuisine to ensure optimal flavor and uncompromised nutritional value.

Beyond captivating recipes, this cookbook also outlines essential information on celiac disease and how to effectively navigate its challenges. The book delves into identifying hidden sources of gluten, understanding food labeling regulations, and finding trustworthy gluten-free products. Moreover, it provides practical advice on maintaining a balanced lifestyle while coping with the emotional aspects of living with celiac disease.

With this invaluable guide by your side, you can confidently transform your kitchen into a haven of deliciousness that satisfies both your taste buds and nutritional needs – leading you on the path towards better health and well-being.

CHAPTER 1: EMBRACING GLUTEN-FREE COOKING

To embrace gluten-free cooking is to prioritize your health and well-being. For individuals with celiac disease, eliminating gluten from the diet is not an option but a necessity. Even for those who are simply choosing to exclude gluten due to personal preferences or intolerances, adopting a gluten-free approach can lead to improved digestion and overall health. Embracing this dietary challenge may at first seem daunting, but once you discover all the incredible alternatives available, your culinary possibilities truly become endless.

Discovering Gluten-Free Alternatives

The first step on this journey is learning about the plethora of wheat alternatives out there. You might be surprised by how many grains, flours, and starches can easily replace wheat in both savory and sweet recipes:

1. **Rice:** Brown or white rice varieties serve as excellent recipe bases for pilafs and risottos.
2. **Quinoa:** Rich in protein and fiber, quinoa is an excellent addition to salads or as a side dish.
3. **Millet:** This small, nutrient-dense grain can be cooked similarly to rice.
4. **Buckwheat:** Despite its name, buckwheat is entirely gluten-free! It forms an excellent base for pancakes and waffles.
5. **Cornmeal:** Use this versatile ingredient to make cornbread or polenta.
6. **Almond flour:** Best for pastries and baked goods, almond flour adds a nutty depth of flavor.
7. **Coconut flour:** Perfect for sweets, coconut flour lends moisture to recipes.
8. **Tapioca starch:** A go-to thickener for sauces and gravies without altering the flavor.

Understanding Celiac Disease

Celiac disease, also known as coeliac disease, is an autoimmune disorder that affects the small intestine and is triggered by the consumption of gluten. Gluten is a protein found in barley, wheat, or rye. When people with celiac disease ingest gluten, it causes their immune system to attack and damage the villi, which are tiny hair-like projections in the small intestine responsible for nutrient absorption. This damage can lead to severe nutritional deficiencies and various health complications.

Symptoms of celiac disease can vary greatly among individuals. Some people may not even experience any clear symptoms at all. Common symptoms include digestive issues such as abdominal pain, bloating, diarrhea, and constipation; weight loss; anemia (due to iron deficiency); fatigue; skin rashes (known as dermatitis herpetiformis); and joint pain.

There are also several more severe complications if celiac disease is left untreated. These include osteoporosis (due to decreased calcium absorption), infertility and miscarriages, neurological disorders like epilepsy and migraines, and increased risk of other autoimmune diseases like type 1 diabetes or multiple sclerosis.

Diagnosis of celiac disease often involves blood tests to detect certain antibodies that are produced in response to gluten exposure. In some cases, an intestinal biopsy may be performed to confirm the presence of damage to the villi. To get accurate results from these tests, it is essential for individuals to keep consuming gluten-containing foods until after their testing is complete.

The only effective treatment for celiac disease is a strict lifelong gluten-free diet. This requires eliminating all sources of gluten from one's diet and opting for naturally gluten-free foods like fruits, vegetables, meats, fish, dairy products (if tolerated), nuts, seeds, legumes, and grains such as rice or quinoa. Many processed foods now offer gluten-free alternatives; however, it is crucial to read labels carefully to avoid inadvertent exposure to gluten. Over time, as the small intestine heals, most people with celiac disease experience improvement or complete resolution of their symptoms and can maintain their health by adhering to a gluten-free diet.

Overcoming Gluten-Free Cooking Challenges: Tips for Success

Embarking on a gluten-free journey can be intimidating at first, but armed with information and a positive attitude, many individuals can quickly become adept at gluten-free cooking. In this chapter, you will learn how to overcome common challenges people face when adapting to a gluten-free diet and how to transform your kitchen into a safe culinary haven.

1. Identifying Hidden Sources of Gluten: One of the most significant challenges in preparing gluten-free meals is recognizing hidden sources of gluten in ingredients. In addition to the well-known sources like wheat, barley, and rye, gluten can be lurking in various sauces, spices, and even beverages.

To overcome this challenge, always read food labels meticulously and look for products that are explicitly labeled as gluten-free. Educate yourself on alternative names for gluten-containing ingredients: malt extract or flavoring, hydrolyzed vegetable protein, and modified food starch often contain gluten.

2. Cross-Contamination Prevention: Cross-contamination refers to the unintended transfer of gluten-containing particles to gluten-free foods. This is a critical issue for people with celiac disease who need to avoid even trace amounts of gluten.

To prevent cross-contamination in your kitchen:

- Designate separate cutting boards, utensils, and cookware for preparing gluten-free foods.
- Always clean surfaces thoroughly before preparing a meal.

- Store your gluten-free ingredients separately from others to avoid contamination.

If using shared appliances such as toasters or ovens, use foil or parchment paper to protect your food.

3. Finding Suitable Substitutes: Luckily, there are now many high-quality gluten-free alternatives available in stores, such as gluten-free flours, pastas, and breads. Experimenting with different brands and recipes can help you find the ones that best mimic the texture and taste of their gluten-containing counterparts. Additionally, utilizing naturally gluten-free foods like rice, potatoes, and quinoa can expand your repertoire of safe and delicious meals.

4. Mastering Gluten-Free Baking: Baked goods can often be a challenge when following a gluten-free diet, as gluten provides structure, elasticity, and texture. Keep these tips in mind while baking:

- Combine different gluten-free flours to achieve desired tastes and textures.
- Incorporate xanthan or guar gum for added structure.
- Add extra liquid or eggs to compensate for the low moisture content of gluten-free flours.
- Allow batter or dough to rest before baking for best results.

5. Expanding Your Recipe Repertoire: To maintain variety in your diet, experiment with new recipes that feature naturally gluten-free ingredients. Explore different cuisines with inherently gluten-free dishes, such as Thai or Indian cuisine.

Use online resources, attend workshops or cooking classes, and share information with fellow chefs in the gluten-free community. This wealth of knowledge will help keep your meals interesting, healthy, and delicious.

While there are challenges in maintaining a gluten-free lifestyle, overcoming these obstacles can provide individuals with celiac disease or gluten sensitivity a chance at improved health and well-being. By mastering your gluten-free cooking skills and continually expanding your recipe collection, you can confidently tackle any culinary challenge that comes your way.

CHAPTER 2:
BREAKFAST BONANZA

1. Quinoa Breakfast Bowl with Fresh Berries

Preparation time: 10 minutes
Cooking time: 15 minutes
Servings: 4

Ingredients:

- One cup uncooked quinoa, washed & strained
- Two cups water
- One tbsp honey
- One tsp vanilla extract, pure
- Quarter tsp cinnamon, ground
- Salt, as required
- One tbsp diced fresh strawberries
- One cup fresh blueberry
- One cup fresh raspberry
- Half cup sliced almonds or chopped nuts

Directions:

1. Mix rinsed quinoa plus water in your saucepan, and let it boil at moderate-high temp.
2. Once boiling, adjust to low temp, cover, then simmer within fifteen minutes till quinoa becomes fluffy. Remove, then let it sit for five minutes before fluffing.
3. Mix in honey, vanilla, cinnamon, plus salt. Top with strawberries, blueberries, raspberries, and sliced almonds when serving.

Nutritional Values (per serving): Calories: 350; Carbs: 60g; Fat: 10g; Protein: 13g; Fiber: 10g

NOTES

_____

_____

_____

2. Gluten-Free Maple Pancakes

Preparation time: 15 minutes
Cooking time: 5 minutes
Servings: 4

Ingredients:

- One & half cups gluten-free flour, all-purpose
- Two tbsp sugar, granulated
- Two tsp baking powder
- Half a tsp salt
- One and a quarter cups almond milk
- One big egg, lightly beaten
- Three tbsp vegetable oil, plus more for the pan
- Half a tsp pure vanilla extract
- Four tbsp pure maple syrup for serving

Directions:

1. Whisk glutenflour, sugar, baking powder, plus salt in your big container.
2. Mix almond milk, lightly beaten egg, oil, and vanilla extract in another container. Mix it with the dry mixture till blended.
3. Warm up your nonstick skillet at moderate temp and lightly coat it with vegetable oil.
4. Pour enough batter, then cook within two to three mins till slightly set. Flip, then cook within one to two minutes till golden brown.
5. Repeat using rest of batter until all pancakes are cooked. Serve warm with maple syrup drizzled on top.

Nutritional Values (per serving): *Calories: 408; Carbs: 62g; Fat: 15g; Protein: 8g; Fiber: 2g*

NOTES

_____

_____

3. Spinach Mushroom Quiche

Preparation time: 20 minutes
Cooking time: 45 minutes
Servings: 6

Ingredients:

- Two tbsp olive oil
- One small chopped onion
- Two cloves of minced garlic
- Eight ounces of button mushrooms, thinly sliced
- Ten ounces of fresh spinach, roughly chopped
- One & half cups cheddar cheese, shredded
- Six big eggs, beaten
- One tbsp milk, any variety (dairy-free if needed)
- Half tsp sea salt
- Quarter tsp black pepper
- One nine-inch gluten-free pie crust, unbaked

Directions:

1. Warm up your oven to 350°F.
2. Warm up oil in your big skillet at moderate temp. Put onion plus garlic, then cook till softened. Put mushrooms, then cook till tender. Put spinach, then cook till wilted.
3. Combine cheddar cheese, eggs, milk, salt, and pepper in your big container. Mix in cooled spinach plus mushroom mixture. Pour it into your pie crust evenly.
4. Bake within 45 minutes till golden brown. Cool it down, slice, then serve.

Nutritional Values (per serving): Calories: 420; Carbs: 24g; Fat: 28g; Protein: 20g; Fiber: 2g

NOTES

----

4. Sweet Potato and Turkey Hash with Poached Eggs

Preparation time: 20 minutes
Cooking time: 30 minutes
Servings: 4

Ingredients:

- One-pound ground turkey
- Two medium-sized sweet potatoes, peeled and diced
- One chopped medium-sized onion
- Two cloves of minced garlic
- One red bell pepper, chopped
- One tbsp olive oil
- Half tsp each paprika & dried thyme
- Salt & pepper, as required
- Four big eggs for poaching

Directions:

1. Heat one tbsp oil in your big skillet at moderate temp.
2. Put chopped onions, bell pepper, plus garlic, then cook till onions become translucent.
3. Add ground turkey, breaking it until browned. Stir in diced sweet potatoes, paprika, dried thyme, salt, plus pepper.
4. Meanwhile, let your pot of water simmer. Crack each egg into a separate small dish or cup.
5. Gently pour each egg into the simmering water one at a time while gently stirring the water around each egg. Cook for 3-4 minutes for soft-poached eggs or adjust to desired doneness.
6. Remove eggs, then put on top of cooked turkey and sweet potato hash. Serve.

Nutritional Values (per serving): *Calories: 400; Carbs: 30g; Fat: 20g; Protein: 30g; Fiber: 5g*

NOTES

_____

_____

5. Veggie and Goat Cheese Frittata

Preparation time: 15 minutes
Cooking time: 25 minutes
Servings: 6

Ingredients:

- Six big eggs
- One cup packed chopped baby spinach leaves
- One medium each diced red bell pepper & grated zucchini
- One small chopped onion
- Two cloves of minced garlic
- Four ounces of goat cheese, crumbled
- Two tbsp olive oil
- One tsp basil, dried
- Salt & pepper, as required

Directions:

1. Warm up your oven to 375°F. Whisk eggs, dried basil, salt, plus pepper in your big container. Put aside.
2. Warm up oil in your oven-safe skillet at moderate temp. Put onion, then cook within five minutes till softened.
3. Put garlic, red bell pepper, plus zucchini, then cook within five minutes till tender. Mix in chopped spinach until just wilted.
4. Pour egg mixture, then gently stir. Sprinkle crumbled goat cheese on top. Move the skillet to your oven, then bake within twenty minutes till the frittata is cooked. Remove, cool it down, then slice. Serve.

Nutritional Values (per serving): Calories: 250; Carbs: 6g; Fat: 19g; Protein: 14g; Fiber: 2g

NOTES

---

6. Banana Almond Pancakes

Preparation time: 10 minutes
Cooking time: 15 minutes
Servings: 4

Ingredients:

- Two ripe bananas, mashed
- One & half cups almond flour
- Half cup unsweetened almond milk
- Two big eggs
- One tbsp honey
- One tsp each vanilla extract & baking powder
- Quarter tsp salt
- Extra virgin olive oil, as needed
- **For serving:** Sliced almonds, fresh fruit, maple syrup (optional)

Directions:

1. In your container, combine mashed bananas, almond flour, almond milk, eggs, honey, vanilla extract, baking powder, plus salt till smooth.
2. Warm up your non-stick skillet at moderate temp and coat it using olive oil.
3. Pour enough batter, then cook within two mins till slightly set. Flip, then cook within one to two minutes till golden brown.
4. Repeat with rest of batter until all pancakes are cooked. Serve warm topped with optional toppings.

Nutritional Values (per serving): Calories: 390; Carbs: 27g; Fat: 28g; Protein: 14g; Fiber: 6g

NOTES

---

7. Quinoa & Berry Parfait

Preparation time: 15 minutes
Cooking time: 20 minutes
Servings: 4

Ingredients:

- One cup quinoa, uncooked
- Two cups water
- One tsp vanilla extract
- Half tsp cinnamon
- One and a half cups mixed berries (e.g., strawberries, raspberries, blueberries)
- Two cups of Greek yogurt or your favorite dairy-free yogurt
- Four tbsp honey or maple syrup
- Quarter cup almond slices, toasted

Directions:

1. In your medium saucepan, add quinoa plus water. Let it boil at moderate temp. Once boiling, adjust to low temp and cover the saucepan.
2. Cook within 15 to 20 minutes until thoroughly cooked, then fluff it with your fork. Mix in vanilla and cinnamon.
3. Prepare the parfait by layering your glass or jar of cooked quinoa, a layer of yogurt, a spoonful of honey, a layer of mixed berries, then sprinkle toasted almond slices. Repeat for each serving.

Nutritional Values (per serving): Calories 375; Carbs 53g; Fat 10g; Protein 18g; Fiber 6g

NOTES

_____

_____

_____

8. Greek Yogurt & Granola Bowl

Preparation time: 10 minutes
Cooking time: 0 minutes
Servings: 2

Ingredients:

- One cup gluten-free granola
- Two cups of Greek yogurt (plain or flavored, as desired)
- One tbsp honey
- Half a tbsp mixed fresh berry (blueberries, strawberries, raspberries)
- Quarter cup chopped almonds
- Quarter cup unsweetened shredded coconut

Directions:

1. Place one tbsp Greek yogurt in each serving bowl. Sprinkle half a tbsp gluten-free granola over the yogurt in each bowl.
2. Divide the mixed fresh berries between the two bowls, placing them on the granola. Drizzle one tbsp honey evenly over the two bowls.
3. Add one-eighth of a tbsp chopped almonds and one-eighth of a tbsp unsweetened shredded coconut to each bowl, evenly distributing the ingredients. Serve.

Nutritional Values (per serving): Calories: 480; Carbs: 55g; Fat: 20g; Protein: 25g; Fiber: 9g

NOTES

_____

_____

_____

9. Waffles with Blueberry Compote

Preparation time: 15 minutes
Cooking time: 20 minutes
Servings: 4

Ingredients:

- Two cups gluten-free flour
- One tbsp granulated sugar
- One tbsp baking powder
- Half a tsp salt
- One and three-quarter cups of almond milk
- Quarter cup melted coconut oil
- Two big eggs
- One tsp pure vanilla extract

For Blueberry Compote:

- Two cups of fresh or frozen blueberries
- Quarter cup water
- Two tbsp honey or maple syrup

Directions:

1. Whisk gluten-free flour, sugar, baking powder, plus salt in your big container.
2. Mix milk, coconut oil, eggs, and vanilla in your separate container. Combine it with the dry mixture till blended.
3. Warm up your waffle iron, then lightly grease it using non-stick spray.
4. Pour about half a cup batter into your waffle iron, then cook till crispy.
5. While the waffles are cooking, prepare the blueberry compote by adding the blueberries, water, and honey (or maple syrup) to a saucepan at a moderate temp.
6. Cook within 10 minutes till blueberries have softened and thickened. Serve the waffles with warm blueberry compote drizzled on top.

Nutritional Values (per serving): Calories: 450; Carbs: 60g; Fat: 20g; Protein: 8g; Fiber: 5g

NOTES

_____

_____

10. Fruit & Nut Breakfast Bars

Preparation time: 15 minutes
Cooking time: 25 minutes
Servings: 12 bars

Ingredients:

- Two cups of rolled oats, gluten-free
- One cup chopped mixed nuts (almonds, walnuts, and pecans)
- Half cup dried mixed fruit (raisins, cranberries, and apricots)
- Half cup unsweetened shredded coconut
- Quarter cup chia seeds
- Quarter cup sunflower seeds
- One tbsp cinnamon
- Half tsp sea salt
- Half cup almond butter
- Half cup honey
- One tsp vanilla extract, pure

Directions:

1. Warm up your oven to 350°F. Line your eight-by-eight inch baking dish using baking paper.
2. Mix gluten-free rolled oats, mixed nuts, dried fruit, shredded coconut, chia seeds, sunflower seeds, cinnamon, and sea salt in your big container.
3. In your microwavable container, warm up almond butter plus honey for 30 seconds till they are easily mixed. Add vanilla, then mix well.
4. Pour it on the rolled oats mixture, then stir gently. Press it firmly into your baking dish using your hands.
5. Bake for 25 minutes till golden brown. Cool it down, remove, slice, then serve.

Nutritional Values (per serving): *Calories: 292; Carbs: 34g; Fat: 15g; Protein: 7g; Fiber: 5g*

NOTES

_____

_____

11. Avocado & Poached Egg on Toast

Preparation time: 10 minutes
Cooking time: 5 minutes
Servings: 2

Ingredients:

- Two big cage-free eggs
- One ripe avocado, halved & pitted
- Two slices of gluten-free bread toasted
- One tbsp white vinegar
- One tbsp lemon juice
- Salt & pepper, as required
- **Optional garnishing:** red pepper flakes, chopped cilantro

Directions:

1. Boil your pot (filled with about 3 inches of water) with a tbsp vinegar. Crack one egg into your small container or ramekin.
2. Gently pour the egg into your pot, then poach within five minutes. Remove, then put aside on your paper towel-lined plate. Repeat with the second egg.
3. Scoop out avocado flesh into your container, then mash it lightly. Add lemon juice, salt, plus pepper. Spread it onto each slice of toast.
4. Gently put one poached egg on top. Sprinkle with red pepper flakes and chopped cilantro if desired. Serve.

Nutritional Values (per serving): Calories: 270; Carbs: 17g; Fat: 19g; Protein: 9g; Fiber: 7g

NOTES

----

12. Coconut Chia Pudding with Mango Puree

Preparation time: 10 minutes + chilling time
Cooking time: 0 minutes
Servings: 4

Ingredients:

- One & a half cups of gluten-free coconut milk
- One-third cup chia seeds
- Two tbsp honey
- One tsp vanilla extract, pure
- Half a tsp cinnamon, ground
- Salt, as required
- Two cups of ripe mango chunks (one big or two small mangos)
- Two tsp fresh lime juice

Directions:

1. Mix gluten-free coconut milk, chia seeds, honey, vanilla, cinnamon, and salt in your medium container. Cover, then refrigerate within two hours till the chia pudding has thickened.
2. While the chia pudding is chilling, prepare the mango puree by blending the mango chunks and lime juice until smooth.
3. To serve, evenly layer the chia pudding with the mango puree in each glass or bowl. You can spoon the portions into each glass or use a piping bag to create neat layers. Serve.

Nutritional Values (per serving): Calories: 295; Carbs: 34g; Fat: 15g; Protein: 6g; Fiber: 9g

NOTES

_____

_____

_____

13. Almond Flour Blueberry Muffins

Preparation time: 15 minutes
Cooking time: 25 minutes
Servings: 12 muffins

Ingredients:

- Two and a half cups of almond flour
- One tsp baking soda
- A quarter tsp sea salt
- Three big eggs
- One-third cup honey
- Two tbsp melted coconut oil
- One tbsp lemon juice
- One tsp vanilla extract
- One tbsp blueberries, fresh

Directions:

1. Warm up your oven to 350°F. Line your muffin tin using 12 paper liners.
2. Mix almond flour, baking soda, plus sea salt in your medium container.
3. Whisk eggs, honey, coconut oil, lemon juice, and vanilla in your separate container. Combine it with the flour mixture till blended. Fold in blueberries.
4. Distribute it among your muffin cups. Bake within 22-25 mins till golden brown. Cool it down, then serve.

Nutritional Values (per serving): *Calories: 119; Carbs: 15g; Fat: 14g; Protein: 7g; Fiber: 3g*

NOTES

_____

_____

_____

14. Gluten-Free Veggie Sausage Skillet

Preparation time: 15 minutes
Cooking time: 20 minutes
Servings: 4

Ingredients:

- Four gluten-free veggie sausages
- Two cups diced potatoes
- One big chopped green & red bell pepper,
- One medium-sized chopped onion
- Two cloves minced garlic
- One tbsp halved cherry tomatoes
- Half tsp each smoked paprika & ground cumin
- Salt & pepper, as required
- Two tbsp olive oil

Directions:

1. Warm up one tbsp oil in your big skillet at moderate temp. Cook gluten-free veggie sausages till browned. Remove, then put aside.
2. Add remaining oil to your skillet. Add potatoes, then cook within 10 minutes till they become tender and lightly browned.
3. Add bell peppers, onion, plus garlic, then cook within 5 minutes till softened. Mix in cherry tomatoes, smoked paprika, plus ground cumin; cook for two more minutes.
4. Chop the cooked veggie sausages and add them back into the skillet. Cook within three minutes till heated through. Flavor it using salt plus pepper. Serve.

Nutritional Values (per serving): *Calories: 375; Carbs: 30g; Fat: 20g; Protein: 18g; Fiber: 5g*

NOTES

_____

_____

15. Gluten-Free Bagels with Smoked Salmon

Preparation time: 30 minutes
Cooking time: 25 minutes
Servings: 6

Ingredients:

- Three cups gluten-free flour, all-purpose
- Two tsp xanthan gum
- One tbsp sugar
- One tsp salt
- One & quarter cups warm water
- One packet of active dry yeast (7 grams)
- Two tbsp vegetable oil
- One tbsp apple cider vinegar
- Six ounces of smoked salmon
- Four ounces of cream cheese softened (use dairy-free if needed)
- Half cup sliced cucumber
- Half sliced small red onion
- Two tbsp capers drained
- Fresh dill sprigs for garnish

Directions:

1. Combine gluten-free flour, xanthan gum, sugar, and salt in your big container. Put aside.
2. In another container, mix warm water and active dry yeast. Put aside within five minutes. Add vegetable oil and apple cider vinegar to the yeast mixture.
3. Slowly pour it into your flour mixture, mixing till you have a dough. Cover your dough using plastic wrap, then let it rise within 1 hour.
4. Warm up your oven to 400°F. Line your baking sheet using baking paper. Split your dough into six, then shape them into bagels.
5. Place the bagels onto your baking sheet, then bake within 25 mins golden brown. Cool slightly before slicing in half horizontally.
6. Spread each bagel half with cream cheese. Top with smoked salmon, cucumber slices, red onion, capers, and fresh dill.

Nutritional Values (per serving): Calories: 450; Carbs: 65g; Fat: 15g; Protein: 15g; Fiber: 5g

NOTES

CHAPTER 3:
SATISFYING STARTERS

16. Grilled Lemon Herb Shrimp Skewers

Preparation time: 20 minutes

Cooking time: 6-8 minutes

Servings: 4

Ingredients:

- One pound of big peeled shrimp
- Quarter cup olive oil
- Juice of one lemon
- Two cloves minced garlic
- One tbsp each chopped parsley & cilantro, fresh
- One tsp dried oregano
- One tsp cumin, ground
- Half tsp smoked paprika
- Salt & black pepper, as required

Directions:

1. Whisk oil, juice, garlic, parsley, cilantro, oregano, cumin, smoked paprika, salt, and pepper in your medium container. Mix in shrimp to the marinade, then refrigerate within 15 minutes.
2. Preheat your grill to moderate-high temp. Thread the shrimp onto your soaked bamboo skewers (approximately four shrimp per skewer).
3. Grill the shrimp skewers on each side for three to four minutes until pink. Serve.

Nutritional Values (per serving): *Calories: 270; Carbs: 3g; Fat: 14g; Protein: 32g; Fiber: 0g*

NOTES

_____

_____

_____

17. Buffalo Chicken Wings with Ranch Dressing

Preparation time: 15 minutes
Cooking time: 45 minutes
Servings: 4

Ingredients:

- Two pounds of chicken wings (split at the joint)
- One tbsp olive oil
- One tsp powdered garlic
- One tsp powdered onion
- One tsp paprika
- One tsp salt
- Half tsp black pepper
- Half cup gluten-free buffalo wing sauce
- Two tbsp unsalted butter, melted

For the Ranch Dressing:

- Half cup gluten-free mayonnaise
- Half cup sour cream
- One tbsp fresh lemon juice
- Two tsp dill weed, dried
- Two tsp parsley dried
- One tsp powdered garlic
- One tsp powdered onion
- Salt & black pepper, as required

Directions:

1. Warm up your oven to 400°F. Line your baking sheet using baking paper.
2. Add oil, powdered garlic, powdered onion, paprika, salt, and black pepper in your big container. Add chicken wings, then toss until evenly coated.

3. Arrange the chicken wings on your baking. Bake within forty minutes until crispy, turning halfway through cooking.

4. While the wings are baking, prepare the ranch dressing by whisking together mayonnaise, sour cream, lemon juice, dill weed, parsley, powdered garlic, powdered onion, salt, and black pepper in your small container. Chill until needed.

5. In another container, combine melted butter and buffalo wing sauce. Toss cooked wings in the buffalo sauce mixture until coated. Serve it with ranch dressing on the side.

Nutritional Values (per serving): Calories: 576; Carbs: 6g; Fat: 47g; Protein: 30g; Fiber: 1g

NOTES

_____

_____

_____

18. Baked Garlic Parmesan Chicken Tenders

Preparation time: 15 minutes
Cooking time: 20 minutes
Servings: 4

Ingredients:

- One pound no bones & skin chicken tenders
- One cup grated Parmesan cheese
- One cup almond flour
- One tsp powdered garlic
- One tsp powdered onion
- One tsp dried each oregano & basil
- Half tsp salt
- Quarter tsp black pepper, ground
- Two big eggs, beaten

Directions:

1. Warm up your oven to 400°F. Line your baking sheet using baking paper.
2. Mix grated Parmesan cheese, almond flour, powdered garlic, powdered onion, oregano, basil, salt, and ground black pepper in your shallow container.
3. In another shallow container, whisk eggs until well beaten.
4. Dip each chicken tender into your egg mixture, then roll it in Parmesan-almond flour mixture.
5. Place each coated chicken tender on the prepared baking sheet, spacing them evenly. Bake within twenty mins. Serve.

Nutritional Values (per serving): Calories 430; Carbs 11g; Fat 24g; Protein 46g; Fiber 3g

NOTES

----

19. Zucchini Fritters with Yogurt Sauce

Preparation time: 15 minutes
Cooking time: 20 minutes
Servings: 4

Ingredients:

- Two medium-sized zucchinis, grated
- One cup all-purpose flour, gluten-free
- One tsp baking powder
- Half tsp salt
- Quarter tsp black pepper, ground
- One big egg, lightly beaten
- Half cup crumbled feta cheese
- Two tbsp chopped fresh dill
- Two tbsp olive oil

For the Yogurt Sauce:

- One cup Greek yogurt, plain
- Half cup chopped mint leaves, fresh
- Two cloves of minced garlic
- Salt & black pepper, as required

Directions:

1. Mix grated zucchini, flour, baking powder, salt, plus black pepper in your big container. Mix in beaten egg, feta cheese, plus chopped dill until combined.
2. Heat olive oil in your big skillet at moderate temp.
3. Scoop spoonfuls of the zucchini mixture into the skillet, flattening each fritter slightly. Cook for three to four minutes per side until crisp.
4. Meanwhile, mix yogurt, mint leaves, garlic, salt, plus pepper in your small container. Serve the zucchini fritters warm with a side of yogurt sauce.

Nutritional Values (per serving): Calories: 370; Carbs: 42g; Fat: 16g; Protein: 14g; Fiber: 3g

NOTES

----

20. Gluten-Free Spinach & Artichoke Dip

Preparation time: 10 minutes
Cooking time: 25 minutes
Servings: 8

Ingredients:

- One (fourteen-oz) can artichoke hearts, strained, chopped
- One (ten-oz) package of spinach, chopped & squeezed excess liquid
- One cup Parmesan cheese, grated
- One cup shredded mozzarella cheese
- One cup sour cream
- Half cup mayonnaise
- Two cloves of minced garlic
- Half tsp salt
- Quarter tsp black pepper

Directions:

1. Warm up your oven to 350°F.
2. Mix artichoke hearts, spinach, Parmesan cheese, mozzarella cheese, sour cream, mayonnaise, garlic, salt, plus black pepper in your big container. Stir until well combined.
3. Transfer it to your oven-safe baking dish. Bake within 25 minutes till the dip is bubbly. Serve with gluten-free crackers or vegetables.

Nutritional Values (per serving): *Calories: 281; Carbs: 6g; Fat: 25g; Protein: 9g; Fiber: 2g*

NOTES

---

21. Creamy Avocado Hummus with Veggie Sticks

Preparation time: 10 minutes
Cooking time: 0 minutes
Servings: 4

Ingredients:

- One ripe avocado, peeled & remove seed
- One & a half cups of cooked chickpeas (canned works fine)
- Quarter cup tahini
- Quarter cup fresh lemon juice
- Two cloves of minced garlic
- Three tbsp olive oil, extra-virgin
- One-half tsp cumin, ground
- Salt & black pepper, as required
- Veggie sticks (carrots, cucumbers, bell peppers, celery)

Directions:

1. Blend avocado, chickpeas, tahini, juice, garlic, oil, plus cumin until smooth in your processor. Add salt and black pepper.
2. Once the hummus is creamy and smooth, transfer it to a serving container. Serve with various veggie sticks.

Nutritional Values (per serving): Calories: 320; Carbs: 28g; Fat: 18g; Protein: 8g; Fiber: 8g

NOTES

_____

_____

_____

22. Crunchy Baked Lentil Chips

Preparation time: 15 minutes
Cooking time: 25 minutes
Servings: 6

Ingredients:

- Two cups red lentils (rinsed and drained)
- Half cup tapioca starch
- One tsp salt
- Quarter tsp powdered onion
- Quarter tsp powdered garlic
- Half a tsp ground cumin
- Quarter tsp ground paprika
- Two tbsp olive oil
- Three-quarters of a tbsp water

Directions:

1. Warm up your oven to 350°F. Line two baking sheets using baking paper.
2. In your blender, blend the red lentils to form a fine flour. Transfer to your big container.
3. Mix tapioca starch, salt, powdered onion, garlic, cumin, and paprika into your lentil flour. Mix in olive oil and water until smooth.
4. Spread it evenly onto your baking sheets, about 1/8 inch thick.
5. Bake within fifteen minutes, remove, then slice the partially baked mixture into desired chip shapes.
6. Bake again within ten minutes until crisp. Remove, then cool it down. Serve.

Nutritional Values (per serving): Calories: 240; Carbs: 39g; Fat: 6g; Protein: 11g; Fiber: 5g

NOTES

----

23. Herbed Sweet Potato Fries

Preparation time: 10 minutes
Cooking time: 30 minutes
Servings: 4

Ingredients:

- Two big sweet potatoes sliced into fries
- Two tbsp olive oil
- Half tsp salt
- Quarter tsp ground black pepper
- One tbsp rosemary, fresh, chopped
- One tbsp thyme, fresh, chopped
- **Optional:** one-half tsp powdered garlic (ensure it is gluten-free)

Directions:

1. Warm up your oven to 425°F.
2. In your big container, mix sweet potato fries, oil, salt, pepper, rosemary, thyme, plus powdered garlic (if using).
3. Arrange the seasoned sweet potato strips on your baking paper-lined baking sheet.
4. Bake within fifteen minutes, flip the fries, then bake again for fifteen minutes till crispy. Cool it down. Serve.

Nutritional Values (per serving): Calories: 236; Carbs: 28g; Fat: 10g; Protein: 2g; Fiber: 5g

NOTES

----

24. Gluten-Free Pita Chips

Preparation time: 10 minutes
Cooking time: 15 minutes
Servings: 4

Ingredients:

- Four pita breads, gluten-free, sliced into triangles
- Quarter cup olive oil, extra virgin
- One tsp powdered garlic
- Half tsp powdered onion
- One tsp dried oregano
- One tsp dried basil
- Salt, as required

Directions:

1. Warm up your oven to 375°F.
2. Mix oil, powdered garlic, powdered onion, dried oregano, and dried basil in your small container.
3. Brush each pita triangle with the olive oil mixture, ensuring an even side coating. Sprinkle salt to taste.
4. Arrange them on your baking sheet. Bake within twelve minutes until crispy, rotating your baking sheet once. Remove, then cool it down. Serve.

Nutritional Values (per serving): Calories 310; Carbs 35g; Fat 16g; Protein 6g; Fiber 3g

NOTES

_____

_____

_____

25. Cheesy Cauliflower Tots

Preparation time: 15 minutes
Cooking time: 20 minutes
Servings: 4

Ingredients:

- One big cauliflower head cut into florets
- Half cup shredded cheddar cheese
- Quarter cup almond flour
- One big egg, beaten
- One tsp each powdered garlic & powdered onion
- Half a tsp salt
- Quarter tsp black pepper

Directions:

1. Warm up your oven to 400°F. Line your baking sheet using baking paper.
2. Steam your cauliflower florets within 5 minutes until tender. Cool slightly.
3. Squeeze out the cauliflower using your cheesecloth as much excess water as possible.
4. Mix squeezed cauliflower, shredded cheddar cheese, almond flour, beaten egg, powdered garlic, powdered onion, salt, and pepper in your big container.
5. Form the mixture into small tot-shaped pieces, then put them on your baking sheet. Bake within twenty mins until crispy. Serve.

Nutritional Values (per serving): Calories 155; Carbs 8g; Fat 11g; Protein 7g; Fiber 3g

NOTES

_____

_____

_____

CHAPTER 4:
WHOLESOME SOUPS
AND SALADS

26. Roasted Creamy Vegetable Soup

Preparation time: 15 minutes
Cooking time: 45 minutes
Servings: 6

Ingredients:

- Two peeled & chopped big carrots
- One medium zucchini, chopped
- One each chopped (yellow & red) bell peppers, & red onion
- Four cups of gluten-free chicken or vegetable broth
- One cup canned full-fat coconut milk
- One tbsp olive oil
- Half a tbsp thyme, dried
- Half a tbsp rosemary, dried
- Salt & black pepper, as required

Directions:

1. Warm up your oven to 425°F.
2. On your big baking sheet, spread bell peppers, carrots, zucchini, and onion in an even layer. Drizzle it with oil. Toss in dried thyme, rosemary, salt, plus black pepper.
3. Roast within 25 minutes till it is tender. Move them to your big pot along with the broth.
4. Let it boil at a moderate-high temp, then simmer within 15 minutes. Add canned coconut milk, mix well, then cook for five minutes.
5. Carefully blend it using your immersion blender till smooth. Serve hot.

Nutritional Values (per serving): Calories: 250; Carbs: 21g; Fat: 14g; Protein: 7g; Fiber: 5g

NOTES

_____

_____

_____

27. Thai Coconut Curry Pumpkin Soup

Preparation time: 15 minutes
Cooking time: 30 minutes
Servings: 6

Ingredients:

- Two tbsp coconut oil
- One chopped medium onion
- Three minced cloves of garlic
- Two cups of pureed pumpkin
- Two cups of vegetable broth
- One 13.5-ounce can of coconut milk, full-fat
- One tbsp gluten-free Thai red curry paste
- One tbsp freshly squeezed lime juice
- One tbsp gluten-free soy sauce (tamari)
- Half tsp ground ginger
- Half tsp salt
- Quarter tsp black pepper

Directions:

1. In your big pot, warm up oil at moderate temp. Add the onion, then cook for three to five mins. Add garlic, then cook for one minute.
2. Mix in pureed pumpkin, broth, coconut milk, plus Thai red curry paste. Mix in lime juice, gluten-free soy sauce (tamari), ground ginger, salt, and black pepper.
3. Let it boil, adjust to low temp, then simmer within twenty minutes. Serve.

Nutritional Values (per serving): Calories: 260; Carbs: 17g; Fat: 21g; Protein: 3g; Fiber: 3g

NOTES

----

28. Chilled Avocado Cucumber Soup

Preparation time: 15 minutes + chilling time
Cooking time: 0 minutes
Servings: 4

Ingredients:

- Two medium-sized cucumbers, peeled, seeded, and roughly chopped
- One ripe, pitted & scooped avocado
- One cup Greek yogurt, plain (dairy-free if desired)
- One small garlic clove, minced
- One tbsp freshly squeezed lime juice
- Two tbsp fresh dill, chopped
- Two cups cold water
- Salt & pepper, as required

Directions:

1. Mix chopped cucumbers, avocado, Greek yogurt, minced garlic, lime juice, and fresh dill in your blender. Blend until smooth.
2. Gradually add the cold water while blending. Flavor the soup using salt and pepper.
3. Chill the soup in your refrigerator. Serve cold, garnished with additional chopped dill if desired.

Nutritional Values (per serving): Calories: 160; Carbs: 12g; Fat: 10g; Protein: 7g; Fiber: 3g

NOTES

_____

_____

_____

29. Hearty Lentil & Vegetable Stew

Preparation time: 15 minutes
Cooking time: 43 minutes
Servings: 6

Ingredients:

- One cup green lentils, thoroughly washed
- Four cups vegetable broth (make sure it's gluten-free)
- Two tbsp olive oil
- One big onion, finely chopped
- Two minced cloves of garlic
- Two medium carrots, diced
- Two stalks of celery, chopped
- One small zucchini, diced
- One red bell pepper, diced
- One and a half cups diced tomatoes (canned or fresh)
- Half a tsp dried thyme
- Half a tsp dried oregano
- Salt & black pepper, as required

Directions:

1. In your big pot, heat olive oil at moderate temp. Put onion and garlic, then cook for five mins.
2. Put carrots plus celery, then cook for five mins. Mix in zucchini, bell pepper, tomatoes, thyme, oregano, salt, plus black pepper. Cook for another three to four minutes.
3. Put lentils plus vegetable broth into your pot, then let it boil. Simmer within thirty to forty minutes. Serve.

Nutritional Values (per serving): Calories: 210; Carbs: 33g; Fat: 6g; Protein: 12g; Fiber: 9g

NOTES

----

30. Butternut Squash and Cauliflower Bisque

Preparation time: 15 minutes

Cooking time: 40 minutes

Servings: 6

Ingredients:

- One medium peeled & cubed butternut squash
- One medium head of cauliflower, sliced into florets
- One diced yellow onion
- Two cloves minced garlic
- Four cups vegetable broth
- One tbsp olive oil
- Half tsp cumin, ground
- Quarter tsp nutmeg, ground
- Salt & black pepper, as required

Directions:

1. In your big pot, warm up the oil at a moderate temp. Add the diced onion, then cook for three to four minutes. Add minced garlic, then sauté for one to two minutes.
2. Mix in butternut squash, cauliflower, vegetable broth, cumin, and nutmeg. Let it boil, adjust to low temp, then simmer within thirty minutes till butternut squash and cauliflower are tender.
3. Remove the vegetables, then blend using your immersion blender until smooth. Warm it up gently on low temp before serving. Flavor it using salt plus black pepper.

Nutritional Values (per serving): Calories: 130; Carbs: 21g; Fat: 4g; Protein: 2g; Fiber: 4g

NOTES

_____

_____

_____

31. Quinoa and Black Bean Salad with Lime Dressing

Preparation time: 20 minutes
Cooking time: 15 minutes
Servings: 4

Ingredients:

- One cup quinoa, washed & strained
- Two cups water
- One bay leaf
- One can (around 15 ounces) black beans, strained & washed
- One big red bell pepper, diced
- One chopped medium red onion
- One cup corn kernels
- Half cup chopped cilantro
- Quarter cup olive oil, extra-virgin
- Four tbsp lime juice
- One tsp ground cumin
- Half tsp chili powder
- Salt & ground black pepper, as required

Directions:

1. In your pot, let quinoa, water, plus bay leaf boil. Adjust to low temp, cover, then simmer within 15 minutes till quinoa is cooked. Discard bay leaf, then fluff the quinoa.
2. Let the quinoa cool slightly and transfer it to your big container.
3. Add bell pepper, black beans, onion, corn kernels, plus chopped cilantro.
4. Whisk oil, juice, cumin, chili powder, salt, plus pepper in your small container. Pour it into your salad mixture. Mix well. Serve.

Nutritional Values (per serving): Calories 410; Carbs 52g; Fat 14g; Protein 13g; Fiber 10g

NOTES

----

32. Kale and Quinoa Salad with Lemon Vinaigrette

Preparation time: 20 minutes
Cooking time: 20 minutes
Servings: 4

Ingredients:

- One cup uncooked quinoa, washed & strained
- Two cups water
- Four cups chopped kale (stems removed), massage to soften
- One medium diced red bell pepper
- Half of a chopped red onion, small
- One big avocado, cubed
- Half cup dried cranberry

For the Lemon Vinaigrette:

- Quarter cup lemon juice, fresh
- Quarter cup olive oil, extra virgin
- Salt & pepper, as required

Directions:

1. In your saucepan, boil two cups of water. Add quinoa, adjust to low temp, cover, then simmer within fifteen minutes until quinoa becomes fluffy. Put aside.
2. Mix juice, oil, salt, plus pepper in your small container.
3. Mix cooked quinoa, prepared kale, diced bell pepper, chopped onion, cubed avocado, and cranberries in your big container. Pour the lemon vinaigrette, then mix well. Serve.

Nutritional Values (per serving): Calories: 450; Carbs: 60g; Fat: 20g; Protein: 12g; Fiber: 9g

NOTES

----

33. Grilled Chicken & Strawberry Spinach Salad

Preparation time: 20 minutes
Cooking time: 10 minutes
Servings: 4

Ingredients:

- Four no bones & skin chicken breasts
- One tbsp olive oil, extra-virgin
- One tsp salt
- Half-tsp black pepper, ground
- Eight cups of baby spinach, fresh
- Two cups sliced strawberries
- One cup halved cherry tomatoes
- A quarter tbsp toasted sliced almond

For the Dressing:

- A quarter tbsp olive oil, extra-virgin
- Two tbsp balsamic vinegar
- One tbsp honey
- One tsp Dijon mustard (ensure gluten-free)
- Salt & black pepper, as required

Directions:

1. Warm up your grill to moderate-high heat.
2. Rub chicken breasts with the one tbsp oil, then flavor using salt and pepper.
3. Grill chicken within five minutes per side until cooked. Remove, then cool it down before slicing.

In your small container or jar, whisk or shake together the dressing Ingredients: oil, vinegar, honey, mustard, salt, plus pepper. Put aside.

4. Mix spinach, strawberries, cherry tomatoes, and toasted almonds in your big container. Add the sliced grilled chicken on top. Drizzle dressing, then serve.

Nutritional Values (per serving): Calories 450; Carbs 22g; Fat 28g; Protein 32g; Fiber 5g

NOTES

_____

_____

34. Zesty Lime & Shrimp Salad

Preparation time: 15 minutes
Cooking time: 5 minutes
Servings: 4

Ingredients:

- One-pound peeled shrimp
- Two tbsp olive oil
- One tsp each & paprika ground cumin
- Salt & pepper, as required
- Four cups of mixed greens
- Two big ripe avocados, diced
- One cup halved cherry tomatoes
- Half a small sliced red onion
- Quarter cup chopped cilantro
- One jalapeno, seeded and thinly sliced (optional)

For the zesty lime vinaigrette:

- Four tbsp fresh lime juice
- One tsp honey
- One clove of minced garlic
- Half tsp ground cumin
- Salt & pepper, as required
- Three to four tbsp olive oil, extra virgin

Directions:

1. Combine shrimp, oil, cumin, paprika, salt, and pepper in your medium container.
2. Heat your big skillet on moderate-high temp. Cook shrimp for two to three minutes per side till opaque. Put aside.
3. To prepare the zesty lime vinaigrette, whisk lime juice, honey, garlic, cumin, salt, plus pepper in your small container. Gradually add oil while whisking till the dressing is well combined.

4. In a big serving container, arrange mixed greens, diced avocado, cherry tomatoes, sliced red onion, chopped cilantro, and jalapeno if using. Top with the cooked shrimp.
5. Drizzle the zesty lime vinaigrette, then mix well. Serve.

Nutritional Values (per serving): *Calories: 399; Carbs: 17g; Fat: 28g; Protein: 24g; Fiber: 8g*

NOTES

_____

_____

_____

35. Asian Green Bean & Sesame Salad

Preparation time: 15 minutes
Cooking time: 5 minutes
Servings: 4

Ingredients:

- One pound fresh green beans trimmed
- Two tbsp gluten-free tamari sauce
- Two tbsp rice vinegar
- One tbsp sesame oil
- One tsp grated ginger
- Two cloves of minced garlic
- Half tsp red pepper flakes, crushed
- Two tbsp toasted sesame seeds
- A quarter tbsp sliced green onions

Directions:

1. Boil your big pot with water. Put green beans, then cook for four mins till crisp-tender. Strain, then wash.
2. Mix tamari sauce, rice vinegar, oil, ginger, garlic, plus crushed red pepper flakes in your small container. Whisk well to create the dressing.
3. Add the cooled green beans, toasted sesame seeds, and sliced green onions in your big container. Pour the dressing on top, then mix well. Serve.

Nutritional Values (per serving): Calories: 130; Carbs: 14g; Fat: 7g; Protein: 4g; Fiber: 4g

NOTES

_____

_____

_____

CHAPTER 5:
DELECTABLE
MAIN COURSES

36. Spinach and Feta Stuffed Chicken Breast

Preparation time: 20 minutes
Cooking time: 30 minutes
Servings: 4

Ingredients:

- Four no bones & skin chicken breasts
- One cup chopped spinach, fresh
- One cup feta cheese, crumbled
- Half cup diced red bell pepper
- One tbsp minced garlic
- One tbsp olive oil
- Half tsp each & dried oregano & black pepper
- Quarter tsp salt

Directions:

1. Warm up your oven to 375°F.
2. Mix chopped spinach, crumbled feta cheese, diced red bell pepper, and minced garlic in your medium container.
3. Using your sharp knife, make a pocket slit in each chicken breast. Stuff each chicken with spinach and feta mixture.
4. Mix oil, oregano, black pepper, and salt in your small container. Rub it onto each chicken breast.
5. Put stuffed chicken breasts on your parchment-lined baking tray. Bake within thirty mins thirty mins till cooked. Serve.

Nutritional Values (per serving): Calories: 310; Carbs: 7g; Fat: 16g; Protein: 36g; Fiber: 1g

NOTES

----

37. Cauliflower Crust Margherita Pizza

Preparation time: 15 minutes
Cooking time: 35 minutes
Servings: 4

Ingredients:

- One medium cauliflower head sliced into florets
- One cup part-skim mozzarella cheese, grated
- Two big eggs, beaten
- One tsp dried oregano
- One tsp powdered garlic
- Half tsp kosher salt
- One cup marinara sauce
- One cup halved cherry tomatoes
- Two cups fresh basil leaves
- Quarter cup Parmesan cheese, grated

Directions:

1. Warm up your oven to 425°F. Line your pizza tray using baking paper. Add cauliflower to your processor, then pulse till it reaches a rice-like consistency.
2. Move it to your microwave-safe container, then microwave for five minutes to soften. Cool it down. Put cooled cauliflower rice in your kitchen towel and squeeze it out.
3. Mix cauliflower rice, mozzarella, eggs, oregano, powdered garlic, plus salt in your big container to create the crust dough.
4. Spread the dough onto the parchment-lined tray, forming an even layer about a quarter-inch thick. Bake the crust for twenty minutes until fully cooked.
5. Remove, then evenly spread the marinara sauce on top. Sprinkle cherry tomatoes, fresh basil leaves, and Parmesan on the sauce.
6. Bake within ten mins till toppings are heated. Remove, cool it down, and then slice. Serve.

Nutritional Values (per serving): Calories 365; Carbs 20g; Fat 18g; Protein 28g; Fiber 7g

NOTES

_____

_____

38. Gluten-Free Pasta Alfredo with Broccoli

Preparation time: 10 minutes
Cooking time: 20 minutes
Servings: 4

Ingredients:

- Eight ounces gluten-free fettuccine pasta
- Four cups broccoli florets
- One tbsp olive oil
- Three cloves minced garlic
- One & half cups heavy cream
- One cup parmesan cheese, grated
- Salt & pepper, as required

Directions:

1. Boil your big pot with salted water, then cook pasta till tender. Add the broccoli in the last three minutes. Strain, then put aside.
2. Meanwhile, warm up the oil in your big skillet at moderate temp. Add garlic, then cook for one minute.
3. Pour heavy cream, then simmer within five minutes. Stir in grated parmesan cheese until thoroughly melted and combined with the heavy cream. Flavor it using salt plus pepper.
4. Add cooked pasta and broccoli, mixing well. Serve.

Nutritional Values (per serving): Calories: 610; Carbs: 43g; Fat: 39g; Protein: 20g; Fiber: 3g

NOTES

_____

_____

_____

39. Baked Lemon and Herbs Cod

Preparation time: 15 minutes
Cooking time: 20 minutes
Servings: 4

Ingredients:

- Four (6-oz) cod fillets
- Two tbsp olive oil
- One big lemon, sliced
- Two tbsp fresh parsley chopped
- Two cloves of minced garlic
- One tsp each dried thyme & oregano
- Half a tsp salt
- A quarter tsp black pepper

Directions:

1. Warm up your oven to 400°F. Grease your baking dish using oil. Put cod fillets in your baking dish, then drizzle them with one tbsp olive oil.
2. Mix garlic, thyme, oregano, salt, and pepper in your small container. Sprinkle it evenly on each fillet—lay lemon slices on the seasoned cod fillets.
3. Bake for 15-20 minutes till the cod flakes easily. Serve.

Nutritional Values (per serving): Calories: 223; Carbs: 4g; Fat: 8g; Protein: 33g; Fiber: 1g

NOTES

_____

_____

_____

40. Pesto Zucchini Noodles

Preparation time: 15 minutes
Cooking time: 10 minutes
Servings: 4

Ingredients:

- Four medium spiralized zucchinis
- One cup fresh basil leaves packed
- One clove garlic
- Quarter cup pine nuts toasted
- One-half cup grated Parmesan cheese
- Salt & pepper, as required
- One-third cup olive oil, extra-virgin
- One tbsp lemon juice, fresh
- Half cup cherry tomatoes, halved (optional)

Directions:

1. In your processor, process basil, garlic, pine nuts, Parmesan cheese, salt, plus pepper until finely chopped.
2. While it's running, gradually pour oil, then blend until smooth. Add juice, then blend again briefly.
3. At moderate temp, cook the zucchini noodles in your big skillet for three to five minutes.
4. Remove, then toss with the prepared pesto sauce. Mix well to coat all noodles evenly. Top with cherry tomatoes if desired. Serve.

Nutritional Values (per serving): Calories: 350; Carbs: 12g; Fat: 30g; Protein: 10g; Fiber: 4g

NOTES

_____

_____

_____

41. Grilled Chimichurri Steak

Preparation time: 15 minutes
Cooking time: 10 minutes
Servings: 4

Ingredients:

- Four six-ounce beef steaks (sirloin or ribeye)
- One tsp sea salt
- One tsp black pepper
- Two cups fresh parsley, finely chopped
- Half cup fresh cilantro, finely chopped
- Two garlic cloves, minced
- One small red chili pepper, minced (optional)
- One tsp dried oregano
- Half cup olive oil, extra-virgin
- Quarter cup red wine vinegar
- One tbsp lemon juice, fresh

Directions:

1. Warm up your grill to moderate-high temp. Flavor the steaks using sea salt and black pepper.
2. In your container, mix parsley, cilantro, garlic, red chili pepper (if using), oregano, oil, vinegar, and juice to make the chimichurri sauce. Mix well and set aside.
3. Grill the steaks within 4-5 minutes per side until cooked. Remove the steaks, then let them rest within 5 minutes to redistribute their juices.
4. Serve the grilled steaks with a generous topping of chimichurri sauce.

Nutritional Values (per serving): *Calories: 550; Carbs: 3g; Fat: 41g; Protein: 45g; Fiber: 1g*

NOTES

---

42. Quinoa Stuffed Bell Peppers

Preparation time: 20 minutes
Cooking time: 45 minutes
Servings: 4

Ingredients:

- Four big bell peppers, sliced tops & seeded
- One cup cooked quinoa
- Two tbsp olive oil
- One small chopped onion
- Two cloves of minced garlic
- One medium zucchini, diced
- One cup chopped mushrooms
- Half cup halved cherry tomatoes
- One cup canned black beans strained & washed
- Salt & pepper, as required
- One tsp smoked paprika
- One tsp cumin powder

Directions:

1. Warm up your oven to 350°F.
2. Add olive oil, followed by the chopped onion plus garlic, in your big skillet on moderate temp. Cook within five minutes.
3. Add diced zucchini, chopped mushrooms, cherry tomatoes, and black beans. Cook within five minutes.
4. Mix in cooked quinoa, paprika, and cumin powder. Flavor it using salt and pepper. Put bell peppers on your baking dish with their sliced tops beside them.
5. Fill each pepper with the prepared mixture till full. Cover, then bake within 25 minutes. Uncover, then cook within ten mins till bell peppers are tender. Serve.

Nutritional Values (per serving): Calories: 320; Carbs: 45g; Fat: 10g; Protein: 12g; Fiber: 7g

NOTES

_____

_____

43. Chicken and Vegetable Stir-Fry

Preparation time: 15 minutes
Cooking time: 10-15 minutes
Servings: 4

Ingredients:

- One pound no bones & skin bite-sized chicken breasts
- Two tbsp soy sauce, gluten-free
- Two tbsp hoisin sauce, gluten-free
- One tbsp honey
- One tbsp cornstarch
- Quarter cup water
- Two tbsp vegetable oil
- One clove of minced garlic
- One tsp grated ginger, fresh
- One cup broccoli florets
- One cup sliced bell peppers (any color)
- Half cup sliced carrots
- Half cup chopped green onions

Directions:

1. Whisk soy & hoisin sauce, honey, cornstarch, and water in your small container. Put aside.
2. Warm up one tbsp oil in your big skillet on moderate-high temp. Add garlic plus ginger, then cook within 30 seconds, mixing.
3. Add chicken, then cook for five minutes until cooked through. Remove the chicken, then put aside.
4. Add remaining oil to your skillet. Cook broccoli, bell peppers, plus carrots within three minutes. Mix in green onions and cooked chicken.
5. Pour the sauce mixture on top, then cook within two minutes till the sauce has thickened and fully coats everything. Serve.

Nutritional Values (per serving): Calories 301; Carbs 17g; Fat 11g; Protein 31g; Fiber 2g

NOTES

_____

_____

44. Meatballs with Marinara Sauce

Preparation time: 15 minutes
Cooking time: 30 minutes
Servings: 4

Ingredients:

- One pound turkey or beef, ground
- One-third cup gluten-free breadcrumbs
- Quarter cup Parmesan cheese, grated
- Quarter cup chopped parsley, fresh
- Half tsp oregano, dried
- Half tsp salt
- Quarter tsp black pepper
- One beaten egg
- Two cups marinara sauce (gluten-free)
- Two tbsp olive oil

Directions:

1. Combine ground meat, breadcrumbs, Parmesan, oregano, parsley, salt, black pepper, and egg in your big container.
2. Shape the mixture into one-and-a-half-inch meatballs, then put them on a plate or tray.
3. Heat olive oil in your big skillet at moderate temp. Add the meatballs, then cook for ten minutes, turning often till browned. Remove the meatballs, then put aside.
4. Add gluten-free marinara sauce in your same skillet at low temp and allow it to simmer within five minutes. Add the meatballs, cover, then cook within ten minutes. Serve.

Nutritional Values (per serving): Calories: 341; Carbs: 16g; Fat: 20g; Protein: 26g; Fiber: 3g

NOTES

----

45. Lemon Herb Roasted Chicken

Preparation time: 20 minutes
Cooking time: 1 hour & 30 minutes
Servings: 4

Ingredients:

- One whole chicken (four pounds)
- Two lemons, zested and juiced
- Four cloves of minced garlic
- One tbsp chopped each rosemary, & thyme (fresh)
- One tsp chopped oregano, fresh
- One tsp paprika
- Half cup olive oil
- Salt & pepper, as required

Directions:

1. Warm up your oven to 425°F.
2. Mix lemon zest, lemon juice, minced garlic, chopped rosemary, thyme, oregano, paprika, olive oil, salt, plus pepper in your small container.
3. Remove the giblets from your chicken, then clean the inside using cold water. Pat dry using paper towels.
4. Put chicken in your roasting pan. Rub the herb mixture all over your chicken, getting it under the skin and inside the cavity.
5. Truss the chicken by tying the legs with kitchen twine, then tucking the wings under its body.
6. Roast for approximately 1 hour and 30 minutes, basting periodically with pan juices. Remove, then cool it down before carving.

Nutritional Values (per serving): Calories: 470; Carbs: 3g; Fat: 32g; Protein: 42g; Fiber: 0.5g

NOTES

_____

_____

46. Baked Dill and Lemon Salmon

Preparation time: 10 minutes

Cooking time: 20 minutes

Servings: 4

Ingredients:

- Four (six-oz) salmon fillets
- One tbsp olive oil, extra-virgin
- Half tsp sea salt
- Quarter tsp black pepper
- One lemon, thinly sliced
- Two tbsp fresh dill, chopped
- One clove of garlic, minced

Directions:

1. Warm up your oven to 375°F. Line your baking sheet using baking paper.
2. Mix oil, salt, black pepper, plus garlic in your small container. Put salmon fillets on your baking sheet, then brush the prepared mixture on each fillet.
3. Arrange lemon slices on top, then sprinkle with dill. Bake within fifteen mins till salmon flakes easily. Serve.

Nutritional Values (per serving): Calories: 295; Carbs: 2g; Fat: 18g; Protein: 30g; Fiber: 0.5g

NOTES

_____

_____

_____

47. Gluten-Free BBQ Pulled Pork Sandwiches

Preparation time: 20 minutes
Cooking time: 6-8 hours (slow cooker)
Servings: 8

Ingredients:

- Two pounds boneless pork shoulder roast
- One tbsp olive oil
- One big, thinly sliced onion
- Two cloves of minced garlic
- One cup gluten-free barbecue sauce
- Half cup water
- One tbsp apple cider vinegar
- Half tsp each smoked paprika & ground cumin
- Salt & pepper, as required
- Eight gluten-free hamburger buns
- **Optional toppings:** coleslaw, pickles, sliced red onion

Directions:

1. Warm up oil in your big skillet on moderate temp. Season the pork shoulder using salt plus pepper, then cook within three mins per side till browned.
2. Put onion plus garlic in your slow cooker. Put browned pork shoulder on top.
3. Whisk gluten-free barbecue sauce, water, apple cider vinegar, smoked paprika, and ground cumin in your medium container. Pour this mixture over the pork shoulder.
4. Cook for six to eight hours on low till pork is easily shredded. Remove the pork, then shred it. Add it to your slow cooker, then mix well.
5. Toast your gluten-free buns if desired, and fill each with a generous serving of pulled pork. Top with your choice of optional toppings, such as coleslaw, pickles, or sliced red onion.

Nutritional Values (per serving): Calories: 450; Carbs: 45g; Fat: 15g; Protein: 27g; Fiber: 3g

NOTES

----

48. Chicken Lettuce Wraps with Peanut Sauce

Preparation time: 15 minutes
Cooking time: 10 minutes
Servings: 4

Ingredients:

- One pound no bones & skin chicken breasts, diced
- Eight big lettuce leaves
- One medium red bell pepper, thinly sliced
- Half a cup shredded carrot
- Quarter cup chopped green onions
- Two tbsp olive oil
- Salt & pepper, as required

For the Peanut Sauce:

- Half cup gluten-free peanut butter (smooth or chunky)
- Two tbsp tamari soy sauce, gluten-free
- Two tbsp rice vinegar
- One tbsp honey
- One tbsp fresh lime juice
- One clove of garlic, minced

Directions:

1. In your medium container, whisk peanut sauce fixings until smooth. Put aside.
2. In your big skillet on moderate-high temp, add olive oil. Once heated, add the chicken. Flavor it using salt and pepper, then cook within six to eight minutes.
3. Assemble wraps: Lay out each lettuce leaf and evenly distribute the cooked chicken among them. Top each with red bell pepper slices, shredded carrots, and chopped green onions.
4. Drizzle your desired amount of peanut sauce over each wrap. Fold both sides, then roll it up. Serve.

Nutritional Values (per serving): Calories: 435; Carbs: 18g; Fat: 27g; Protein: 33g; Fiber: 4g

NOTES

_____

_____

49. Cauliflower Fried Rice with Shrimp

Preparation time: 15 minutes
Cooking time: 20 minutes
Servings: 4

Ingredients:

- One medium-sized cauliflower, chopped into florets
- Half a pound of peeled & deveined shrimp
- Two tbsp vegetable oil
- One small chopped onion
- Two cloves of minced garlic
- One cup frozen peas and carrots mixture
- Two big eggs, beaten
- Three tbsp gluten-free soy sauce or tamari
- Two green thinly sliced onions
- One tsp sesame oil

Directions:

1. In your processor, pulse the cauliflower florets to reach a rice-like consistency.
2. Warm up one tbsp oil in your big non-stick skillet at moderate temp.
3. Add the shrimp, then cook within two to three minutes per side until pink. Move it to your plate.
4. Add a tbsp oil in your same skillet, then cook onion for two minutes. Add minced garlic, peas, and carrots within three to four minutes.
5. Move them to one side, then pour beaten eggs into the empty side of your skillet. Cook until scrambled.
6. Stir in cauliflower rice and cooked shrimp, mixing well with vegetables and scrambled eggs. Add gluten-free soy sauce , , then cook for three to four minutes.
7. Drizzle sesame oil over the fried rice and garnish with thinly sliced green onions. Serve.

Nutritional Values (per serving): Calories: 270; Carbs: 18g; Fat: 11g; Protein: 23g; Fiber: 5g

NOTES

_____

_____

50. Stuffed Acorn Squash with Quinoa and Cranberries

Preparation time: 20 minutes
Cooking time: 45 minutes
Servings: 4

Ingredients:

- Two medium-sized acorn squashes, halved and seeds removed
- One cup quinoa, rinsed and drained
- Two cups water
- Half cup each dried cranberry, diced celery & chopped toasted pecans
- One small chopped onion
- Two cloves of minced garlic
- One tsp dried sage
- One tbsp olive oil
- Salt & black pepper, as required

Directions:

1. Warm up your oven to 400°F. Put acorn squash halves on your parchment-lined baking sheet. Bake within 25 mins.
2. Meanwhile, in your medium saucepan, boil quinoa and water. Adjust to low temp, cover, then simmer within fifteen minutes until quinoa is cooked.
3. In your big skillet, warm up the oil at moderate temp. Put onion, celery, plus garlic, then cook within five minutes.
4. Mix in cooked quinoa, cranberries, toasted nuts, dried sage, salt, and pepper.
5. Fill each squash with a quinoa mixture. Return the stuffed squash halves to the oven within fifteen mins till heated.

Nutritional Values (per serving): Calories: 450; Carbs: 70g; Fat: 18g; Protein: 10g; Fiber: 9g

NOTES

CHAPTER 6: GLUTEN-FREE BAKING ESSENTIALS

Mastering the basics of gluten-free baking requires an understanding of alternative ingredients, proper techniques, and patience to produce delectable treats without sacrificing taste or texture. Gluten is a protein found in wheat, barley, and rye, giving baked goods their structure and elasticity. It also helps create tender, airy textures in breads and pastries. However, many people experience sensitivities or adverse reactions to gluten, which has led to the increased popularity of gluten-free baking.

A critical element in mastering gluten-free baking is learning to use alternative flours and starches. Some commonly used gluten-free flours include:

1. Almond Flour: Made from ground almonds, this flour is high in protein and natural fats. It works well as a substitute for wheat flour in recipes that require a dense texture, such as cookies or cakes.

2. Coconut Flour: Derived from dried coconut meat, this flour is highly absorbent and low-carb. It's essential to balance moisture levels with extra eggs or liquids when using coconut flour.

3. Rice Flour: Ground from rice grains, rice flour possesses a neutral flavor that works well in various recipes, but can sometimes result in crumbly baked goods due to its lower binding capabilities.

4. Tapioca Flour: Extracted from the cassava plant's roots, tapioca flour offers excellent binding properties and a light texture but lacks nutrients compared to other flours.

5. Buckwheat Flour: Despite its name, buckwheat is unrelated to wheat and is derived from seeds instead of grains. Buckwheat flour provides earthy flavors that pair well with chocolate or nuts.

6. Sorghum Flour: This naturally gluten-free flour made from sorghum grain has a smooth texture and mild flavor. It's ideal for replacing wheat flour in many recipes.

7. Potato Flour: Made from dehydrated potatoes, potato flour is highly absorbent, but excessive amounts can result in gummy textures.

Blending flours can create more balanced flavors, textures, and nutritional profiles in your gluten-free baked goods.

Gluten-Free Baking Techniques

Mastering key techniques is vital to producing delicious gluten-free baked goods. Here are some tips to help:

1. Accurate Measuring: Weighing ingredients with a digital scale ensures precision, especially when working with gluten-free flours that may have varying densities.

2. Adding Gums: Ingredients like xanthan gum or guar gum mimic gluten's binding properties to prevent crumbly textures and improve the rise of your baked goods.

3. Enhancing Flavor: Gluten-free flours often have distinct tastes that you can complement by adding spices or extracts such as cinnamon, nutmeg, or vanilla.

4. Adjusting Baking Time and Temperature: Gluten-free baked goods tend to require longer baking times at lower temperatures due to their higher moisture content and lower protein structure.

5. Cooling Properly: Gluten-free baked goods are more delicate when hot; therefore, cooling on a wire rack allows them to firm up without getting soggy.

Mastering the basics of gluten-free baking involves exploring alternative flours, adjusting techniques, and experimenting with recipes to achieve results that satisfy both taste and texture preferences. With practice and patience, you'll soon discover the flavorful world of gluten-free baking that is available at your fingertips.

51. Chocolate Avocado Mousse

Preparation time: 10 minutes + chilling time
Cooking time: 0 minutes
Servings: 4

Ingredients:

- Two ripe halved & pitted avocados
- One-third cup unsweetened cocoa powder
- Quarter cup honey or maple syrup
- One cup coconut milk
- One tsp vanilla extract, pure
- Sea salt, as required
- Fresh berries, mint leaves, and shredded coconut for garnishing (optional)

Directions:

1. Scoop avocados flesh into your food processor. Add the unsweetened cocoa powder, honey, milk, vanilla, plus salt. Blend all till smooth.
2. Refrigerate the mousse within one hour to allow it to set and thicken.
3. Before serving, stir the mousse briefly to maintain its fluffy consistency. Divide it evenly among four small bowls or dessert dishes.
4. Garnish with fresh berries, mint leaves, and shredded coconut if desired.

Nutritional Values (per serving): Calories: 270; Carbs: 20g; Fat: 20g; Protein: 2.5g; Fiber: 5g

NOTES

_____

_____

_____

52. Flourless Lemon Almond Cake

Preparation time: 20 minutes
Cooking time: 35-40 minutes
Servings: 8

Ingredients:

- One & half cups almond flour (finely ground)
- One cup granulated sugar
- One tsp baking powder
- One tbsp grated lemon zest
- Four big eggs, room temperature, divided
- Half a tsp pure vanilla extract
- One tbsp fresh lemon juice
- Quarter cup butter, unsalted, dissolved & cooled

Directions:

1. Warm up your oven to 350°F. Grease your nine-inch round cake pan, then line it using baking paper.
2. In your big container, combine almond flour, sugar, baking powder, and lemon zest.
3. Separate egg whites from the yolks. Add the yolks into the dry mixture along with vanilla extract, lemon juice, and melted butter. Mix until smooth.
4. Beat egg whites till stiff peaks form in your separate container. Fold it into your batter. Pour batter into your cake pan, then bake within thirty-five minutes. Remove, cool it down, then serve.

Nutritional Values (per serving): Calories: 286; Carbs: 27g; Fat: 17g; Protein: 7g; Fiber: 2g

NOTES

_____

_____

_____

53. Gluten-Free Raspberry Coconut Bars

Preparation time: 15 minutes
Cooking time: 25 minutes
Servings: 12 bars

Ingredients:

- One & half cups rolled oats, gluten-free
- Three fourths cup shredded coconut, unsweetened
- One fourth cup coconut flour
- One third cup coconut oil, melted
- One fourth cup honey
- One tsp vanilla extract, pure
- One cup raspberry preserves (gluten-free and celiac-friendly)
- One fourth cup raspberries, fresh or frozen

Directions:

1. Warm up your oven to 350°F. Line your eight-by-eight-inch square baking pan using baking paper.
2. In your big container, mix gluten-free rolled oats, unsweetened shredded coconut, and coconut flour. Add oil, honey, plus vanilla, then stir until well combined.
3. Press around three fourths of the mixture into your baking pan. Spread raspberry preserves on the oat-coconut base in an even layer.
4. Scatter the fresh or frozen raspberries on top of the jam layer. Sprinkle the remaining oat-coconut mixture over the raspberries as a crumble topping.
5. Bake within twenty-five mins. Cool it down, remove, slice, then serve.

Nutritional Values (per serving): Calories 260; Carbs 31g; Fat 12g; Protein 3g; Fiber 4g

NOTES

_____

_____

_____

54. Fudgy Black Bean Brownies

Preparation time: 15 minutes
Cooking time: 25 minutes
Servings: 16 brownies

Ingredients:

- One & half cups cooked black beans, drained and rinsed
- Three big eggs
- Two tbsp melted coconut oil
- Three-fourths cup unsweetened cocoa powder
- Quarter tsp salt
- One tsp gluten-free vanilla extract
- Three-fourths cup granulated sugar or alternative sweetener equivalent
- Half cup dairy-free chocolate chips, semi-sweet

Directions:

1. Warm up your oven to 350°F. Grease your eight-by-eight-inch baking dish.
2. In your food processor, mix beans, eggs, oil, cocoa, salt, vanilla, and sugar. Process until smooth. Fold in chocolate chips.
3. Pour brownie mixture into your baking dish evenly. Bake within twenty-five mins. Cool it down, remove, slice, then serve.

Nutritional Values (per serving): *Calories: 138; Carbs: 18g; Fat: 7g; Protein: 5g; Fiber: 3g*

NOTES

_____
_____
_____

55. Quinoa Apple Crisp

Preparation time: 20 minutes
Cooking time: 45 minutes
Servings: 6

Ingredients:

- One cup uncooked quinoa, rinsed
- One tbsp ground cinnamon
- Two tsp allspice
- Four big apples, peeled, cored, and thinly sliced
- Half a cup gluten-free rolled oats
- Quarter cup almond flour
- One third cup brown sugar (packed)
- Quarter cup unsalted butter, cut into small pieces
- One tsp vanilla extract

Directions:

1. Warm up your oven to 350°F.
2. In your small saucepan, cook quinoa according to package instructions. Allow it to cool slightly.
3. In your big container, mix cooled quinoa with the cinnamon and allspice. Gently fold in the sliced apples.
4. Spread the quinoa-apple mixture evenly in a greased nine-inch square baking dish.
5. In another container, mix rolled oats, almond flour, plus brown sugar. Add butter plus vanilla extract, then work the butter till crumbly.
6. Sprinkle this topping over the quinoa-apple mixture in the baking dish. Bake within 45 minutes till apples are tender. Remove, cool it down, slice, then serve.

Nutritional Values (per serving): Calories: 300; Carbs: 45g; Fat: 11g; Protein: 5g; Fiber: 7g

NOTES

_____

_____

56. No-Bake Peanut Butter Cookies

Preparation time: 15 minutes + chilling time
Cooking time: 0 minutes
Servings: 12 cookies

Ingredients:

- One cup creamy peanut butter
- Half cup honey
- One tsp pure vanilla extract
- Two cups rolled oats, gluten-free
- One cup shredded coconut, unsweetened
- One third cup chia seeds

Directions:

1. In your big container, combine peanut butter, honey, and vanilla extract. Stir till mixture is smooth.
2. Mix in gluten-free rolled oats, shredded coconut, and chia seeds to the peanut butter mixture. Line your baking tray with wax paper.
3. Form your dough into 12 rounded cookies, then put them on your lined tray. Refrigerate the tray within 30 minutes, or until cookies are firm. Serve.

Nutritional Values (per serving): Calories: 330; Carbs: 32g; Fat: 19g; Protein: 9g; Fiber: 6g

NOTES

_____

_____

_____

57. Easy Blueberry Cheesecake

Preparation time: 15 minutes + chilling time
Cooking time: 45 minutes
Servings: 8

Ingredients:

- One & half cups gluten-free graham cracker crumbs
- Quarter cup melted butter
- Sixteen ounces softened cream cheese
- Half cup sugar, granulated
- Two big eggs
- One tsp vanilla extract, pure
- Three-fourths cup gluten-free sour cream
- One & quarter cups fresh blueberries
- One tbsp cornstarch

Directions:

1. Warm up your oven to 350°F. Grease your eight-inch springform pan.
2. In your medium container, mix cracker crumbs plus butter till crumbly. Press it firmly into your pan.
3. In your big container, beat cream cheese plus sugar till smooth. Add eggs one at a time, beating well, then mix in vanilla plus sour cream.
4. Toss the blueberries with the cornstarch to coat them evenly. Gently fold coated blueberries into the cream cheese mixture.
5. Pour it on the crust, then bake within 45 minutes. Cool it down on your wire rack before refrigerating within 4 hours or overnight. Unmold the chilled cheesecake, then serve.

Nutritional Values (per serving): *Calories: 280; Carbs: 29g; Fat: 16g; Protein: 6g; Fiber: 0.5g*

NOTES

_____

_____

58. Chocolate Dipped Coconut Macaroons

Preparation time: 20 minutes
Cooking time: 25 minutes
Servings: 12

Ingredients:

- Three cups unsweetened shredded coconut
- One cup sweetened condensed milk
- One tsp pure vanilla extract
- Two big egg whites
- Salt, as required
- Six ounces gluten-free dark chocolate, melted

Directions:

1. Warm up your oven to 325°F. Line your baking sheet using baking paper.
2. In your medium container, mix shredded coconut, sweetened condensed milk, plus vanilla.
3. In your separate container, beat egg whites plus salt using your electric mixer on moderate-high setting until stiff peaks form. Carefully fold egg whites into the coconut mixture.
4. Scoop heaping tbsp the mixture onto the prepared baking sheet.
5. Bake within twenty mins till macaroons are slightly golden on top and around the edges. Cool it down.
6. Dip each half of macaroon into your chocolate, then put them back on your parchment paper or silicone mat to set. Allow chocolate to harden before serving.

Nutritional Values (per serving): Calories: 285; Carbs: 18g; Fat: 22g; Protein: 4g; Fiber: 4g

NOTES

----

59. Gluten-Free Maple Pecan Pie Bars

Preparation time: 15 minutes
Cooking time: 45 minutes
Servings: 16 bars

Ingredients:

- One & half cups almond flour
- Quarter cup coconut flour
- One-third cup coconut oil, melted
- One-third cup pure maple syrup, divided
- Half a tsp salt, divided
- One & half cups chopped pecans
- Two big eggs, lightly beaten
- Three-quarters cup coconut sugar
- One tsp pure vanilla extract

Directions:

1. Warm up your oven to 350°F. Grease your eight-by-eight-inch square baking pan, then line it using baking paper.
2. In your medium container, combine almond flour, coconut flour, melted coconut oil, one-quarter cup maple syrup, and one-quarter tsp salt.
3. Press it evenly into your baking pan, then bake within ten mins. Remove, then cool slightly.
4. While crust is cooling, mix together chopped pecans, eggs, coconut sugar, remaining one-quarter tsp salt, and vanilla extract in your separate container.
5. Pour it on cooled crust, then bake within thirty mins till pecan layer is set and slightly puffed. Remove, cool it down, slice, then serve.

Nutritional Values (per serving): Calories: 215; Carbs: 18g; Fat: 15g; Protein: 4g; Fiber: 2g

NOTES

_____

_____

60. Gluten-Free Apple Galette

Preparation time: 20 minutes
Cooking time: 45 minutes
Servings: 6

Ingredients:

- Two cups gluten-free flour, all-purpose
- One cup cold unsalted butter, cubed
- One tsp salt
- Half cup ice water
- Four big apples, peeled, cored, and thinly sliced
- One-third cup granulated sugar
- One tsp ground cinnamon
- Half tsp ground nutmeg
- One tbsp lemon juice
- One egg, lightly beaten with one tbsp water (for egg wash)
- Two tbsp coarse sugar (optional)

Directions:

1. In your big container, mix gluten-free flour, salt, and cold butter. Work the butter till mixture is crumbly.
2. Add ice water gradually, then mix till dough starts to come together. You may not need all of the water.
3. Form your dough into a flat disk, wrap using cling plastic, then chill within one hour. Warm up your oven to 375°F. Line your baking sheet using baking paper.
4. In your big container, mix apple slices, sugar, cinnamon, nutmeg, plus juice.
5. Roll out the dough between two sheets of baking paper. Move it to your baking sheet. Arrange spiced apple slices in a circular pattern on top of your dough.
6. Fold up your dough border on the apple edge, crimping it slightly as you go around. Brush egg wash over folded dough edges and sprinkle coarse sugar on top if desired.
7. Bake within forty-five mins till apples are tender. Cool it down, slice, then serve.

Nutritional Values (per serving): Calories: 395; Carbs: 60g; Fat: 15g; Protein: 5g; Fiber: 4g

NOTES

----

61. Almond Flour Snickerdoodles

Preparation time: 15 minutes
Cooking time: 10 minutes
Servings: 12 cookies

Ingredients:

- One & half cups almond flour
- Half tsp baking soda
- Salt, as required
- Quarter cup melted coconut oil
- One third cup honey
- One tsp vanilla extract, pure
- **For coating:** Two tbsp granulated sugar and one tsp ground cinnamon

Directions:

1. Warm up your oven to 350°F. Line your baking sheet using baking paper.
2. In your big container, whisk almond flour, baking soda, plus salt.
3. In your separate container, mix oil, honey, plus vanilla till smooth. Combine it with flour till blended. Shape your dough into twelve equal-sized balls.
4. In your small container, stir sugar plus cinnamon for coating. Roll each dough ball in it till coated.
5. Put coated dough balls onto your baking sheet and gently press down to flatten slightly. Bake within ten mins till golden brown. Remove, cool it down, then serve.

Nutritional Values (per serving): Calories: 159; Carbs: 13g; Fat: 11g; Protein: 3g; Fiber: 1g

NOTES

_____

_____

_____

62. Coconut Flour Chocolate Cake

Preparation time: 15 minutes
Cooking time: 30 minutes
Servings: 8

Ingredients:

- One cup coconut flour
- Half cup cocoa powder, unsweetened
- One tsp baking soda
- Half tsp salt
- Five big eggs
- One cup almond milk, unsweetened
- Three-quarters cup honey
- Half cup melted coconut oil
- One tbsp pure vanilla extract

Directions:

1. Warm up your oven to 350°F. Line your eight-inch round cake pan using baking paper.
2. In your medium container, sift flour, cocoa, baking soda, plus salt.
3. In your big container, whisk eggs, milk, honey, oil, plus vanilla till smooth. Combine it with flour mixture till blended.
4. Pour it into your cake pan, then bake within thirty mins. Remove, cool it down, then serve.

Nutritional Values (per serving): Calories: 296; Carbs: 31g; Fat: 17g; Protein: 7g; Fiber: 6g

NOTES

_____

_____

_____

63. Strawberry Rhubarb Crumble

Preparation time: 20 minutes
Cooking time: 45 minutes
Servings: 8

Ingredients:

- Two cups strawberries, fresh, hulled & halved
- Two cups rhubarb, chopped into one-inch pieces
- One cup gluten-free flour, all-purpose
- Three-quarters cup sugar, granulated
- Three-quarters cup gluten-free rolled oats
- Half cup light brown sugar, packed
- Half cup unsalted butter, cubed
- One tsp ground cinnamon
- Half tsp kosher salt
- One tbsp corn-starch

Directions:

1. Warm up your oven to 350°F. Grease your eight-by-eight-inch baking dish.
2. In your medium container, mix strawberries, rhubarb, granulated sugar, and cornstarch. Put aside.
3. In another container, mix gluten-free flour, brown sugar, gluten-free rolled oats, cinnamon, and salt. Work in the cubed butter till crumbly.
4. Press half of crumble mixture into your baking dish to form a crust. Pour the strawberry-rhubarb filling on the crust, then spread evenly. Sprinkle remaining crumble mixture on top.
5. Bake within forty-five mins till fruit is bubbling. Cool it down, then serve.

Nutritional Values (per serving): Calories: 325; Carbs: 52g; Fat: 12g; Protein: 4g; Fiber: 3g

NOTES

_____

_____

64. Sticky Rice Mango Pudding

Preparation time: 20 minutes
Cooking time: 45 minutes
Servings: 4

Ingredients:

- One cup glutinous rice
- One and a quarter cups water
- One ripe big mango, peeled, pitted, and cut into thin slices
- One cup coconut milk, full-fat
- Two tbsp brown sugar
- Quarter tsp salt

Directions:

1. In your medium saucepan, mix rinsed rice plus one and quarter cups of water. Let it soak within twenty minutes.
2. Boil the soaked rice and water on high temp. Once boiling, adjust to low temp, then cover. Cook within fifteen mins till rice absorbs all the water.
3. In your small saucepan, mix coconut milk, brown sugar, and salt. Heat on moderate temp until sugar dissolves.
4. Pour half of coconut milk mixture, stirring gently to combine. Let it sit for 10 minutes to absorb the flavors.
5. In serving containers or glasses, layer the soaked sticky rice followed by sliced mangoes on top. Drizzle with remaining coconut milk mixture before serving.

Nutritional Values (per serving): Calories: 354; Carbs: 61g; Fat: 11g; Protein: 5g; Fiber: 2g

NOTES

----

65. Cherry Chia Pudding

Preparation time: 10 minutes + chilling time
Cooking time: 0 minutes
Servings: 4

Ingredients:

- One & half cups unsweetened almond milk
- One third cup chia seeds
- Two cups fresh, pitted cherries
- One tsp vanilla extract
- Two tbsp maple syrup
- Salt, as required

Directions:

1. In your medium container, whisk all fixings except the cherries. Put aside within five mins, then whisk again to ensure there are no chia seed clumps. Cover, then refrigerate within four hours.
2. Once the chia pudding has thickened, stir it well to make sure the texture is consistent.
3. Place one tbsp pitted cherries in your blender, then blend till smooth. Coarsely chop the remaining cherries for topping.
4. To assemble, layer alternating servings of chia pudding and cherry sauce in bowls or glasses. Top each serving with chopped cherries.

Nutritional Values (per serving): *Calories: 250; Carbs: 35g; Fat: 11g; Protein: 5g; Fiber: 10g*

CHAPTER 7:
NOURISHING SNACKS
AND SIDE DISHES

66. Veggie and Cheese Quesadillas

Preparation time: 15 minutes
Cooking time: 10 minutes
Servings: 4

Ingredients:

- Eight corn tortillas
- One cup each mozzarella & cheddar cheese, shredded
- One small sliced each green & red bell pepper
- Half a medium-sized red onion, thinly sliced
- Two cups fresh spinach leaves, washed and drained
- Two tbsp olive oil
- Half tsp each salt & ground black pepper

Directions:

1. Warm up one tbsp oil in your big skillet on moderate temp.
2. Add red and green bell peppers and red onion to the skillet. Flavor is using salt and black pepper. Sauté within 5 minutes.
3. Add spinach leaves, then cook within two mins till spinach has wilted. Remove vegetables, then put aside.
4. On your clean surface, lay out four corn tortillas. Divide both types of cheese evenly among the four tortillas.
5. Top each tortilla with an even amount of the sautéed veggie mixture, followed by another layer of cheese divided evenly among the tortillas. Place another corn tortilla on top of each stack.
6. Warm up remaining oil in your clean skillet on moderate temp. Carefully transfer each quesadilla stack to the hot skillet, cooking one at a time.
7. Cook each quesadilla within 2 to 3 minutes per side till crispy. Serve.

Nutritional Values (per serving): Calories: 380; Carbs: 38g; Fat: 19g; Protein: 16g; Fiber: 5g

NOTES

_____

_____

67. Baked Zucchini Fries with Spicy Aioli

Preparation time: 15 minutes
Cooking time: 25 minutes
Servings: 4

Ingredients:

- Four medium zucchinis, sliced into sticks
- One cup gluten-free all-purpose flour
- One tsp salt
- Half tsp black pepper
- Two big eggs
- One & half cups gluten-free breadcrumbs
- Half cup grated Parmesan cheese

For the Spicy Aioli:

- Half cup mayonnaise
- One tbsp Sriracha hot sauce (or to taste)
- One tsp lemon juice
- One clove garlic, minced

Directions:

1. Warm up your oven to 425°F. Line your baking sheet using baking paper.
2. In your shallow container, mix gluten-free flour, salt, plus pepper. In another shallow container, whisk the eggs.
3. In a third shallow container, combine gluten-free breadcrumbs and Parmesan cheese.
4. Dip zucchini fries in flour mixture, then the eggs, the finally coat them in your breadcrumb mixture.
5. Place coated zucchini fries on your baking sheet, then bake within twenty-five minutes till crispy.
6. While zucchini fries are baking, make the spicy aioli by mixing together mayonnaise, Sriracha hot sauce, lemon juice, and minced garlic in your small container. Serve zucchini fries warm with the spicy aioli.

Nutritional Values (per serving): *Calories: 450; Carbs: 45g; Fat: 22g; Protein: 16g; Fiber: 4g*

NOTES

----

68. Chickpea Flour Crackers

Preparation time: 15 minutes
Cooking time: 20-25 minutes
Servings: 4

Ingredients:

- One & half cups chickpea flour
- Half tsp sea salt
- Quarter tsp powdered onion
- Quarter tsp powdered garlic
- Quarter tsp black pepper
- One tbsp finely chopped rosemary (optional)
- Two tbsp olive oil
- Six tbsp water

Directions:

1. Warm up your oven to 350°F. Line your baking tray using baking paper.
2. In your big container, combine chickpea flour, sea salt, powdered onion, powdered garlic, black pepper, and chopped rosemary if using. Add oil, mixing till mixture is crumbly.
3. Gradually pour in water while stirring until a dough forms. If needed, add an extra tbsp water to get the right consistency.
4. Put dough between two baking paper, then roll it out evenly. Remove the top layer of baking paper, then transfer your dough onto your baking tray.
5. Score lines into your dough for individual crackers. Bake within twenty mins till crisp at the edges. Cool it down, slice, then serve.

Nutritional Values (per serving): Calories: 215; Carbs: 23g; Fat: 11g; Protein: 9g; Fiber: 4g

NOTES

---

69. Blueberry Almond Energy Balls

Preparation time: 15 minutes + chilling time
Cooking time: 0 minutes
Servings: 10 balls

Ingredients:

- One cup gluten-free rolled oats
- Half a cup almond butter (or any nut/seed butter of your choice)
- Quarter cup honey or maple syrup (for a vegan option)
- One-third cup dried blueberries
- One-third cup slivered almonds
- Quarter tsp salt
- Half a tsp vanilla extract
- One tbsp chia seeds

Directions:

1. In your big container, mix gluten-free rolled oats, almond butter, honey or maple syrup, dried blueberries, slivered almonds, salt, vanilla extract, and chia seeds.
2. Roll it into balls, then put them on your parchment-lined tray. Refrigerate your energy balls within one hour to set and firm up before serving.

Nutritional Values (per serving): Calories: 210; Carbs: 24g; Fat: 11g; Protein: 5g; Fiber: 4g

NOTES

_____

_____

_____

70. Vegetable Spring Rolls

Preparation time: 30 minutes
Cooking time: 14 minutes
Servings: 4

Ingredients:

- Eight gluten-free rice paper sheets
- Two cups shredded napa cabbage
- One cup julienned carrots
- One cup julienned bell peppers (multicolored)
- Half a tbsp thinly sliced red onion
- cup tbsp bean sprouts
- One handful chopped fresh cilantro
- One handful chopped fresh mint leaves
- Gluten-free soy sauce, for dipping

Directions:

1. Fill your shallow container with warm water, then submerge each rice paper sheet within ten seconds until slightly softened.
2. Lay a softened rice paper sheet on a flat surface, then arrange each vegetable horizontally in your rice sheet. Fold both side, then roll it up to create a sealed spring roll.
3. Repeat process until all eight spring rolls are assembled. Steam the spring rolls over boiling water within 5-7 minutes, using a steamer basket if possible.
4. Remove from heat and serve immediately with gluten-free soy sauce for dipping.

Nutritional Values (per serving): Calories: 110; Carbs: 23g; Fat: 0.5g; Protein: 3g; Fiber: 3g

NOTES

_____

_____

_____

71. Peanut Butter Rice Cake

Preparation time: 10 minutes
Cooking time: 0 minutes
Servings: 4

Ingredients:

- Four rice cakes
- Half a tbsp unsweetened natural peanut butter
- One big banana, sliced thinly
- One tbsp honey
- Two tbsp chia seeds
- Sea salt, as required

Directions:

1. Arrange the rice cakes on a clean surface or plate. Spread an even layer of peanut butter over each rice cake.
2. Top each rice cake with thin slices of banana. Drizzle honey over the banana slices on each rice cake. Sprinkle chia seeds plus salt on each rice cake. Serve.

Nutritional Values (per serving): *Calories: 260; Carbs: 32g; Fat: 13g; Protein: 7g; Fiber: 5g*

NOTES

_____

_____

_____

72. Roasted Rosemary Sweet Potato Wedges

Preparation time: 15 minutes
Cooking time: 30 minutes
Servings: 4

Ingredients:

- Two big sweet potatoes, sliced into wedges
- Two tbsp olive oil
- One tbsp finely chopped fresh rosemary
- Half tsp sea salt
- Quarter tsp black pepper, ground

Directions:

1. Warm up your oven to 400°F.
2. In your big container, mix oil, fresh rosemary, salt, plus pepper. Add sweet potato wedges, then toss well.
3. Move sweet potato wedges on your parchment-lined baking sheet, then bake for fifteen mins. Flip the wedges, then bake again for fifteen mins till cooked through. Serve.

Nutritional Values (per serving): Calories: 189; Carbs: 27g; Fat: 7g; Protein: 2g; Fiber: 4g

NOTES

_____

_____

_____

73. Spiced Pumpkin Seed Brittle

Preparation time: 10 minutes
Cooking time: 25 minutes
Servings: 8

Ingredients:

- One cup raw pumpkin seeds, hulled
- Half tsp salt
- Quarter tsp ground nutmeg
- Quarter tsp ground cinnamon
- One eighth tsp ground cloves
- Half cup granulated sugar
- Quarter cup honey
- Two tbsp unsalted butter

Directions:

1. Warm up your oven to 350°F. Line your big baking sheet using baking paper. Put it aside.
2. In your container, mix pumpkin seeds, salt, nutmeg, cinnamon, and cloves. Stir well to evenly coat the seeds with spices.
3. In your small saucepan on moderate temp, combine sugar, honey, and butter. Cook, stirring continuously till sugar has dissolved.
4. Remove your saucepan, then pour the sugar mixture on spiced pumpkin seeds. Mix well to ensure that all seeds are coated. Spread it evenly on your baking sheet.
5. Bake within twenty mins till bubbly. Remove, then cool it down. Break into bite-sized pieces, then serve.

Nutritional Values (per serving): Calories: 234; Carbs: 24g; Fat: 14g; Protein: 6g; Fiber: 1g

NOTES

----

74. Oven-Baked Banana Chips

Preparation time: 15 minutes
Cooking time: 2 hours
Servings: 4

Ingredients:

- Four medium ripe bananas, sliced into chips
- One tbsp lemon juice, fresh
- Sea salt, as required
- Half-tsp cinnamon (optional)

Directions:

1. Warm up your oven to 200°F. Line your baking sheet using baking paper.
2. In your small container, mix lemon juice, sea salt, and cinnamon (if using). Dip the banana slices in the lemon juice mixture, then put them on your baking sheet.
3. Bake for one hour, then flip the banana slices over to ensure even cooking. Bake for another hour till banana chips are crisp and golden brown. Remove, cool it down, then serve.

Nutritional Values (per serving): Calories: 99; Carbs: 23g; Fat: 0g; Protein: 1g; Fiber: 3g

NOTES

----

75. Crunchy Chickpea Snack Mix

Preparation time: 15 minutes
Cooking time: 30 minutes
Servings: 6

Ingredients:

- Two cups of canned chickpeas, washed & strained
- One tbsp olive oil, extra virgin
- One tsp each smoked paprika & powdered garlic
- Half tsp each powdered onion, ground cumin, ground turmeric & sea salt
- Quarter tsp black pepper
- One cup raw mixed nuts (such as almonds, cashews, and walnuts)
- Three-fourths cup unsweetened coconut flakes

Directions:

1. Warm up your oven to 375°F. Line your baking sheet using baking paper.
2. In your big container, mix rinsed chickpeas, olive oil, smoked paprika, powdered garlic, powdered onion, cumin, turmeric, salt, plus pepper.
3. Spread it onto your baking sheet, then bake for thirty mins, mixing once. Remove, then cool it down.
4. In your separate container, mix together the raw mixed nuts and unsweetened coconut flakes.
5. Once the chickpeas have cooled down slightly, add them to your container, then mix well. Serve.

Nutritional Values (per serving): Calories: 250; Carbs: 20g; Fat: 14g; Protein: 8g; Fiber: 6g

NOTES

_____
_____
_____

76. Cocoa-Dusted Almonds

Preparation time: 10 minutes
Cooking time: 15 minutes
Servings: 12

Ingredients:

- Two cups whole raw almonds
- One tbsp coconut oil, melted
- Two tbsp cocoa powder, unsweetened
- Two tsp cinnamon
- One tsp vanilla extract, pure
- One-quarter tsp sea salt
- Three tbsp powdered stevia or preferred natural sweetener

Directions:

1. Warm up your oven to 350°F.
2. In your big container, mix melted coconut oil, unsweetened cocoa powder, cinnamon, pure vanilla extract, sea salt, and powdered sweetener.
3. Add the whole raw almonds, then toss till almonds are evenly coated with the cocoa mixture.
4. Spread the coated almonds out on your parchment-lined baking sheet. Roast within ten mins, remove, then cool it down. Serve.

Nutritional Values (per serving): Calories: 161; Carbs: 8g; Fat: 13g; Protein: 6g; Fiber: 5g

NOTES

_____

_____

_____

77. Chocolate Quinoa Crispies

Preparation time: 15 minutes + chilling time
Cooking time: 20 minutes
Servings: 6

Ingredients:

- One cup uncooked quinoa, washed & cooked
- Quarter cup honey
- One third cup unsweetened cocoa powder
- Half cup peanut butter, creamy
- Two tbsp coconut oil, dissolved
- One tsp vanilla extract, pure
- Salt, as required

Directions:

1. Warm up your oven to 350°F.
2. Spread the cooked quinoa onto your parchment-lined baking sheet, then bake within fifteen mins till crispy, mixing occasionally. Remove, then cool it down.
3. In your medium container, combine honey, cocoa powder, peanut butter, melted coconut oil, vanilla extract, plus salt. Add your cooled quinoa crispies, then stir until well-coated.
4. Drop spoonfuls of mixture onto a parchment-lined plate or tray and refrigerate within one hour, or until set. Serve.

Nutritional Values (per serving): *Calories: 320; Carbs: 34g; Fat: 17g; Protein: 10g; Fiber: 4g*

NOTES

----

78. Roasted Parmesan Broccoli Bites

Preparation time: 15 minutes
Cooking time: 20 minutes
Servings: 4

Ingredients:

- Four cups fresh broccoli florets
- One tbsp olive oil
- One tsp powdered garlic
- Half tsp sea salt
- Quarter tsp black pepper
- Half cup Parmesan cheese, grated

Directions:

1. Warm up your oven to 400°F. In your big container, mix broccoli florets, olive oil, powdered garlic, sea salt, plus pepper.
2. Spread it on your parchment-lined baking sheet, then roast within fifteen minutes till broccoli begins to brown slightly.
3. Remove your baking sheet, then sprinkle grated Parmesan cheese evenly over the broccoli florets. Roast again within five minutes till slightly crispy. Remove, cool it down, then serve.

Nutritional Values (per serving): Calories: 150; Carbs: 7g; Fat: 10g; Protein: 9g; Fiber: 3g

NOTES

_____

_____

_____

79. Gluten-Free Teriyaki Tofu Stir-Fry

Preparation time: 15 minutes
Cooking time: 30 minutes
Servings: 4

Ingredients:

- One block (fourteen ounces) tofu, extra-firm, pressed and cubed
- Two tbsp each gluten-free tamari & rice vinegar
- One tbsp each honey & grated fresh ginger
- Two cloves minced garlic
- One tbsp cornstarch
- Three tbsp vegetable oil, divided
- Two cups broccoli florets
- One each yellow & red bell pepper, strips
- One big carrot, thinly sliced diagonally
- Four green onions, chopped
- One tbsp sesame seeds (optional)

Directions:

1. In your medium container, whisk tamari, rice vinegar, honey, ginger, garlic, and cornstarch. Add tofu cubes, then toss well. Put it aside.
2. In your big non-stick skillet, warm up one tbsp oil on moderate-high temp. Remove the tofu from the marinade (reserving marinade), then cook till browned. Remove, then put aside.
3. In your same skillet, add another tbsp oil and cook broccoli florets within 5 minutes tilly start to get tender but still retain some crunch.
4. Add sliced bell peppers plus carrots, then continue stir-frying for three mins till veggies are tender-crisp.
5. Make space in the center of the skillet and add the remaining tbsp vegetable oil along with green onions. Cook within a minute till fragrant.
6. Add reserved marinade to the skillet and cook till sauce thickens, stirring continuously.
7. Return cooked tofu to the skillet and combine with the veggies and sauce until all ingredients are well coated.
8. Finally, sprinkle chopped green parts of green onions and sesame seeds on top if desired. Serve.

Nutritional Values (per serving): Calories: 315; Carbs: 20g; Fat: 20g; Protein: 16g; Fiber: 4g

NOTES

----

80. Roasted Brussels Sprouts with Garlic

Preparation time: 10 minutes
Cooking time: 25 minutes
Servings: 4

Ingredients:

- One & half pounds of Brussels sprouts, trimmed and halved
- Three tbsp olive oil, extra-virgin
- Four cloves minced garlic
- Half tsp sea salt
- Quarter tsp black pepper, ground

Directions:

1. Warm up your oven to 400°F.
2. In your big container, mix trimmed and halved Brussels sprouts, oil, garlic, sea salt, plus pepper. Toss the mixture well to evenly coat the sprouts.
3. Arrange the Brussels sprouts onto your parchment-lined baking sheet. Roast within twenty mins, stirring occasionally for even cooking. Serve.

Nutritional Values (per serving): Calories: 170; Carbs: 15g; Fat: 10g; Protein: 6g; Fiber: 6g

NOTES

----

81. Zesty Lime and Cilantro Coleslaw

Preparation time: 15 minutes + chilling time
Cooking time: 0 minutes
Servings: 6

Ingredients:

- Four cups green cabbage, shredded
- One cup red cabbage, shredded
- One big carrot, grated
- Half a red onion, thinly sliced
- Quarter cup chopped fresh cilantro
- One-third cup mayonnaise (gluten-free if necessary)
- Two tbsp lime juice (approximately one lime)
- One tbsp apple cider vinegar
- One tbsp honey
- Half a tsp ground cumin
- Salt & pepper, as required

Directions:

1. In your big container, mix shredded green cabbage, red cabbage, grated carrot, and thinly sliced red onion.
2. In your smaller container, whisk mayonnaise, lime juice, vinegar, honey, cumin, salt plus pepper.
3. Pour it on the vegetables, then toss well. Stir in the chopped fresh cilantro. Cover, then refrigerate within thirty mins. Serve.

Nutritional Values (per serving): *Calories: 135; Carbs: 10g; Fat: 10g; Protein: 2g; Fiber: 3g*

NOTES

_____

_____

_____

82. Rosemary Garlic Mashed Sweet Potatoes

Preparation time: 15 minutes
Cooking time: 30 minutes
Servings: 4

Ingredients:

- Four medium peeled & cubed sweet potatoes
- One tsp salt
- Half tsp ground black pepper
- Two cloves minced garlic
- Two tbsp fresh rosemary, chopped
- One tbsp extra-virgin olive oil
- Half cup unsweetened almond milk

Directions:

1. Put cubed sweet potatoes in your big pot, then fill with enough water to cover them completely. Let it boil, then simmer within twenty mins till sweet potatoes are fork-tender.
2. In your small pan, warm up oil on moderate temp. Add minced garlic, then cook within one minute till fragrant. Mix in chopped rosemary, then cook within one minute.
3. Strain the sweet potatoes, then return them to your pot. Add garlic-rosemary mixture plus unsweetened almond milk.
4. Mash your sweet potatoes till smooth. Add salt plus pepper. Serve.

Nutritional Values (per serving): *Calories: 215; Carbs: 35g; Fat: 7g; Protein: 3g; Fiber: 5g*

NOTES

_____

_____

_____

83. Cumin Roasted Baby Carrots

Preparation time: 10 minutes
Cooking time: 25 minutes
Servings: 4

Ingredients:

- One pound baby carrots
- Two tbsp olive oil
- One tsp ground cumin
- Half tsp salt
- Quarter tsp black pepper, ground

Directions:

1. Warm up your oven to 400°
2. In your big container, combine olive oil, ground cumin, salt, plus pepper.
3. Add baby carrots, then toss till evenly coated with the cumin mixture. Spread it onto your parchment-lined baking sheet.
4. Roast within 25 mins till tender and slightly caramelized, turning halfway through cooking for even roasting. Remove, cool it down, then serve.

Nutritional Values (per serving): Calories: 120; Carbs: 14g; Fat: 7g; Protein: 1g; Fiber: 4g

NOTES

----

84. Corn and Avocado Salsa Fresca

Preparation time: 15 minutes
Cooking time: 0 minutes
Servings: 4

Ingredients:

- One cup corn kernels
- One ripe avocado, diced
- One medium-sized red onion, finely chopped
- One small jalapeno, seeds removed and finely chopped
- Quarter cup fresh cilantro, chopped
- One tbsp lime juice, fresh
- Salt & pepper, as required

Directions:

1. In your medium container, mix corn kernels, diced avocado, onion, plus jalapeno.
2. Mix in the chopped cilantro, juice, salt plus pepper. Serve.

Nutritional Values (per serving): *Calories: 97; Carbs: 10g; Fat: 6g; Protein: 2g; Fiber: 3g*

NOTES

----

85. Cilantro Lime Quinoa Pilaf

Preparation time: 15 minutes
Cooking time: 25 minutes
Servings: 4

Ingredients:

- One cup uncooked quinoa, washed & strained
- Two cups water
- One tbsp olive oil
- One chopped small red onion
- Two cloves minced garlic
- One medium red bell pepper, diced
- One diced medium zucchini
- One cup corn kernels
- Two tbsp lime juice, fresh
- Half cup cilantro, fresh, chopped
- Half tsp cumin, ground
- Salt & black pepper, as required

Directions:

1. In your medium saucepan, let quinoa plus water boil. Adjust to low temp, cover, then simmer within fifteen mins till tender. Remove, fluff, then put it aside.
2. In your big skillet, warm up oil on moderate temp. Add onion plus garlic, then cook within three mins. Add bell pepper, zucchini and corn, then cook within five mins.
3. Mix in cooked quinoa, lime juice, cilantro and cumin. Flavor is using salt plus black pepper.
4. Cook within two minutes while mixing occasionally until everything is well combined and heated through. Serve.

Nutritional Values (per serving): Calories: 258; Carbs: 41g; Fat: 7g; Protein: 9g; Fiber: 6g

NOTES

_____

_____

CHAPTER 8:
COOKING FOR
SPECIAL OCCASIONS

86. Baked Eggplant Parmesan with Gluten-Free Bread Crumbs

Preparation time: 20 minutes
Cooking time: 40 minutes
Servings: 6

Ingredients:

- Two medium eggplants, sliced into half-inch thick rounds
- One & half cups gluten-free bread crumbs
- One cup grated Parmesan cheese
- Two cups gluten-free marinara sauce
- One tsp salt
- One tsp ground black pepper
- Three big eggs, beaten
- Half cup chopped fresh basil
- Two cups mozzarella cheese, shredded
- Olive oil for frying

Directions:

1. Warm up your oven to 375°F.
2. In your shallow container, mix bread crumbs, Parmesan, salt, plus black pepper. In another shallow container, whisk the eggs.
3. Dip each eggplant slice into your beaten eggs, followed by the breadcrumb mixture, ensuring both sides are well-coated.
4. Fill a big frying pan with enough oil on moderate-high temp. Fry each breaded eggplant slice within two mins per side. Put it aside.
5. Spread one cup marinara sauce on your nine-by-thirteen-inch baking dish.
6. Layer half of eggplant slices on top, then one cup mozzarella and half of the chopped fresh basil.
7. Repeat this process with another layer of eggplant slices, marinara sauce, mozzarella cheese, and basil. Bake within twenty mins till bubbly. Serve.

Nutritional Values (per serving): Calories: 415; Carbs: 35g; Fat: 20g; Protein: 18g; Fiber: 8g

NOTES

----

87. Baked Turkey Meatloaf with Tomato Glaze

Preparation time: 15 minutes
Cooking time: 60 minutes
Servings: 6

Ingredients:

- One & half pounds ground turkey
- Three-fourths cup gluten-free breadcrumbs
- Half cup finely chopped onion
- One-third cup chopped fresh parsley
- One big egg, lightly beaten
- Two cloves minced garlic
- One tsp oregano, dried
- Half tsp salt
- Quarter tsp black pepper
- Half cup ketchup, divided
- One tbsp Worcestershire sauce (gluten-free)
- One tbsp Dijon mustard (gluten-free)

Directions:

1. Warm up your oven to 375°F.
2. In your big container, mix ground turkey, gluten-free breadcrumbs, onion, parsley, egg, garlic, oregano, salt, black pepper, and a quarter tbsp ketchup. Mix well.
3. In your small container, whisk remaining ketchup, Worcestershire sauce, plus Dijon mustard to make the tomato glaze.
4. Transfer the turkey mixture to a 9x5-inch loaf pan, then spread tomato glaze on top. Bake within sixty mins till cooked. Cool it down, slice, then serve.

Nutritional Values (per serving): Calories: 290; Carbs: 19g; Fat: 11g; Protein: 28g; Fiber: 1g

NOTES

_____

_____

88. Chicken Pot Pie with Potato Crust

Preparation time: 20 minutes
Cooking time: 50 minutes
Servings: 6

Ingredients:

- Two cups cooked and cubed chicken breast
- One cup sliced carrots
- One cup frozen peas
- Half a cup diced celery
- Two-thirds cup chopped onions
- One-third cup gluten-free all-purpose flour
- Half tsp salt
- Quarter tsp each black pepper, powdered onion & paprika
- One and a half cups chicken broth (gluten-free)
- Two-thirds cup dairy-free milk alternative (e.g., almond milk)
- Five medium-sized russet potatoes, peeled and thinly sliced

Directions:

1. Warm up your oven to 425°F.
2. In your big saucepan, mix carrots, peas, celery, plus onions on moderate temp. Cook till vegetables are tender, about 10 minutes.
3. In your separate container, mix gluten-free flour, salt, pepper, powdered onion, plus paprika.
4. Gradually stir in chicken broth and dairy-free milk into the vegetable mixture. Cook on moderate temp until thickened.
5. Gently fold in the cooked cubed chicken. Lightly grease a deep pie dish or a round casserole dish.
6. Layer your pie dish with half of potatoes. Pour the chicken and vegetable mixture on top of the potato layer.
7. Finish by layering the remaining potato slices on top of the filling to create a crust. Bake within forty mins till cooked. Cool it down, then serve.

Nutritional Values (per serving): Calories: 320; Carbs: 35g; Fat: 8g; Protein: 26g; Fiber: 4g

NOTES

----

89. Beef and Broccoli Stir-Fry

Preparation time: 15 minutes
Cooking time: 20 minutes
Servings: 4

Ingredients:

- One pound beef sirloin, thinly sliced
- Three cups broccoli florets
- One big onion, thinly sliced
- Two cloves minced garlic
- One tbsp fresh ginger, grated
- Quarter cup soy sauce, gluten-free
- Three tbsp hoisin sauce, gluten-free
- One tbsp cornstarch
- Half a cup water
- Two tbsp vegetable oil

Directions:

1. In your small container, whisk soy & hoisin sauce, cornstarch, and water. Put aside.
2. Warm up one tbsp oil in your big skillet on moderate-high temp. Add thinly sliced beef sirloin, then cook till browned. Remove, then put aside.
3. In your same skillet, add another tbsp of oil on moderate-high temp. Add onion slices, then cook till become soft and translucent. Add garlic plus ginger, then cook within two minutes.
4. Mix in broccoli florets, then cook within three mins. Add the cooked beef, then pour prepared sauce mixture on top.
5. Cook everything together within 2-3 minutes till sauce thicken slightly. Serve.

Nutritional Values (per serving): Calories: 371; Carbs: 17g; Fat: 20g; Protein: 34g; Fiber: 3g

NOTES

----

90. Spaghetti Squash with Bolognese Sauce

Preparation time: 20 minutes
Cooking time: 60 minutes
Servings: 4

Ingredients:

- One big spaghetti squash, halved lengthwise & seeded
- One pound beef or turkey, ground
- One tbsp olive oil
- One diced small onion
- Two cloves minced garlic
- One and a half cups crushed tomatoes
- Half a cup vegetable broth
- One tsp dried each oregano & basil
- Salt & pepper, as required

Directions:

1. Warm up your oven to 375°F. Put squash halves on your parchment-lined baking sheet. Bake within forty mins till tender. Remove, cool it down, then scrape out "spaghetti strands". Move it to your big serving container.
2. Meanwhile, warm up oil in your big skillet on moderate temp. Cook ground meat till browned, breaking it up. Strain excess oil.
3. Add onion plus garlic, then cook within three mins till softened.
4. Mix in tomatoes, vegetable broth, oregano, and basil. Let it simmer on moderate temp for fifteen mins. Flavor it using salt plus pepper.
5. Top spaghetti squash with Bolognese sauce, then garnish with fresh parsley or basil.

Nutritional Values (per serving): *Calories: 341; Carbs: 22g; Fat: 19g; Protein: 25g; Fiber: 6g*

NOTES

---

91. Quinoa and Vegetable Stuffed Peppers

Preparation time: 20 minutes
Cooking time: 50 minutes
Servings: 4

Ingredients:

- Four big bell peppers (assorted colors), sliced tops & seeded
- One cup cooked quinoa
- Two tbsp olive oil
- One small chopped onion
- Two cloves minced garlic
- One medium zucchini, diced
- One medium yellow squash, diced
- Two cups chopped fresh spinach
- One (15 oz) can black beans, washed & strained
- One tsp ground cumin
- Half tsp paprika
- Salt & pepper, as required

Directions:

1. Warm up your oven to 350°F. Stand the peppers upright in your baking dish.
2. In your big skillet, warm up oil on moderate temp. Add onion plus garlic, then cook within five mins till softened.
3. Add zucchini and yellow squash to the skillet. Cook within 5 minutes. Stir in spinach, then cook till wilted.
4. Remove skillet, then mix in cooked quinoa, black beans, cumin, paprika, salt, and pepper. Stuff each bell pepper with quinoa mixture.
5. Cover it using aluminum foil, then bake within thirty mins. Uncover, then bake again within fifteen mins till cooked. Serve hot.

Nutritional Values (per serving): *Calories: 290; Carbs: 46g; Fat: 8g; Protein: 12g; Fiber: 11g*

NOTES

_____

_____

92. Baked Lemon Herb Tilapia

Preparation time: 10 minutes
Cooking time: 20 minutes
Servings: 4

Ingredients:

- Four tilapia fillets (approximately six ounces each)
- Quarter cup gluten-free breadcrumbs
- One tsp each dried basil, dried oregano & paprika
- Half tsp each powdered garlic & powdered onion
- Zest & juice of one lemon
- Two tbsp olive oil
- Salt & pepper, as required

Directions:

1. Warm up your oven to 400°F.
2. In your shallow container, mix gluten-free breadcrumbs, basil, oregano, paprika, powdered garlic, powdered onion, salt, plus pepper.
3. In another shallow container, mix lemon juice, zest, and olive oil.
4. Dip each tilapia fillet into the lemon juice mixture, then then press both sides into the breadcrumb mixture.
5. Put coated tilapia fillets on your parchment-lined baking sheet. Bake within fifteen till tilapia is golden brown. Serve.

Nutritional Values (per serving): *Calories: 226; Carbs: 6g; Fat: 9g; Protein: 31g; Fiber: 1g*

NOTES

_____

_____

_____

93. Cauliflower Mac and Cheese with Gluten-Free Pasta

Preparation time: 10 minutes
Cooking time: 25 minutes
Servings: 4

Ingredients:

- Eight oz gluten-free pasta (such as rice or quinoa-based pasta)
- One small head cauliflower, cut into florets
- Two tbsp unsalted butter
- Two tbsp gluten-free flour, all-purpose
- Two cups whole milk
- One & half cups cheddar cheese, shredded
- Half tsp salt
- Quarter tsp black pepper
- Half tsp powdered garlic
- Quarter cup gluten-free breadcrumbs

Directions:

1. Warm up your oven to 350°F.
2. In your big pot with boiling salted water, cook pasta till tender. Add cauliflower florets, then cook within three minutes. Strain, then put aside.
3. In your medium saucepan, dissolve butter on moderate temp. Mix in flour, then cook within one minute, until it begins to bubble.
4. Slowly whisk in milk until smooth. Cook for approximately 5 minutes, till sauce thickens. Remove, then mix in shredded cheddar cheese, salt, pepper, and powdered garlic.
5. Add cooked pasta plus cauliflower, then stir until well combined. Move it to your greased oven-safe dish, then sprinkle breadcrumbs on top.
6. Bake within twenty mins till top is golden brown. Remove, cool it down, then serve.

Nutritional Values (per serving): Calories: 565; Carbs: 59g; Fat: 26g; Protein: 22g; Fiber: 3g

NOTES

----

94. Quinoa Stuffed Portobello Mushrooms

Preparation time: 15 minutes
Cooking time: 25 minutes
Servings: 4

Ingredients:

- Four big Portobello mushrooms, stems removed
- One cup cooked quinoa
- One red bell pepper, diced
- One small chopped onion
- Two cloves of garlic, minced
- One cup spinach, roughly chopped
- Half cup crumbled feta cheese
- Two tbsp olive oil
- Salt & pepper, as required

Directions:

1. Warm up your oven to 375°F.
2. In your medium skillet, heat one tbsp olive oil on moderate temp. Put onions plus garlic, then cook within three mins.
3. Add bell pepper, then cook within five mins. Mix in chopped spinach till wilted, then remove your skillet.
4. In your big container, mix in cooked quinoa, vegetables from the skillet, crumbled feta cheese, salt, and pepper.
5. Scoop even portions of the quinoa mixture into each Portobello mushroom cap, then move it onto your greased baking sheet.
6. Drizzle the rest of oil on the stuffed mushrooms. Bake within twenty mins till cooked through. Serve.

Nutritional Values (per serving): *Calories: 260; Carbs: 22g; Fat: 14g; Protein: 10g; Fiber: 5g*

NOTES

_____

_____

95. Chicken Enchiladas with Green Sauce

Preparation time: 15 minutes
Cooking time: 40 minutes
Servings: 4

Ingredients:

- One pound of shredded cooked chicken
- Eight gluten-free tortillas
- One & half cups of green enchilada sauce
- One finely chopped medium-sized onion
- One can (four ounces) diced green chilies
- One can (15 ounces) drained and rinsed black beans
- Two tsp ground cumin
- Half a tsp salt
- Two cups shredded Mexican blend cheese, divided
- Half a cup finely chopped fresh cilantro, divided
- Cooking oil spray

Directions:

1. Warm up your oven to 350°F.
2. In your big container, mix shredded chicken, onion, green chilies, black beans, cumin, salt, one tbsp cheese, and half of the chopped cilantro. Mix well.
3. Coat your nine-by-thirteen baking dish using oil spray. Pour half cup green enchilada sauce in it, then spread it evenly.
4. Take one gluten-free tortilla and add about 1/8 of chicken mixture down its center. Roll up, then put it in your baking dish. Repeat with the remaining tortillas.
5. Pour the remaining one cup green enchilada sauce on top. Top with the remaining one cup shredded cheese.
6. Bake within twenty-five mins till heated through. Remove, then cool slightly. Sprinkle with remaining cilantro before serving.

Nutritional Values (per serving): Calories: 648; Carbs: 53g; Fat: 27g; Protein: 44g; Fiber: 12g

NOTES

_____

_____

96. Baked Honey Mustard Pork Chops

Preparation time: 10 minutes
Cooking time: 30 minutes
Servings: 4

Ingredients:

- Four boneless pork chops (about six to eight ounces each)
- Quarter cup gluten-free honey mustard
- Two tbsp olive oil
- One tsp dried each thyme & rosemary
- One-half tsp powdered garlic
- Salt & pepper, as required

Directions:

1. Warm up your oven to 375°F. Grease your baking dish using oil.
2. In your small container, mix honey mustard, olive oil, thyme, rosemary, powdered garlic, salt, and pepper. Mix well.
3. Put pork chops in your baking dish, then brush with honey mustard mixture. Bake within thirty minutes till pork chops are cooked through. Remove, then cool it down. Serve.

Nutritional Values (per serving): Calories: 340; Carbs: 8g; Fat: 16g; Protein: 39g; Fiber: 1g

NOTES

----

97. Chicken Piccata with Capers

Preparation time: 15 minutes
Cooking time: 20 minutes
Servings: 4

Ingredients:

- Four no bones & skin chicken breasts, pounded to a quarter-inch thickness
- One cup gluten-free flour for dredging (e.g., rice flour)
- One tbsp salt
- One tbsp black pepper
- Two tbsp olive oil
- One tbsp butter, unsalted
- Half cup lemon juice, fresh
- Half cup gluten-free chicken stock
- Quarter cup brined capers, rinsed and drained

Directions:

1. In your shallow plate, mix gluten-free flour, salt plus pepper. Warm up oil in your big skillet on moderate temp.
2. Dredge each chicken breast in your seasoned flour mixture, then put it in your skillet.
3. Cook within five minutes per side till browned. Remove the chicken, then put aside.
4. In your same skillet, add butter, lemon juice, chicken stock, and capers. Let it boil while gently scraping any browned bits.
5. Adjust to a simmer, then cook within two minutes till slightly reduced. Add cooked chicken breasts, then cook within two minutes, often spooning sauce on top. Serve.

Nutritional Values (per serving): Calories: 375; Carbs: 30g; Fat: 14g; Protein: 32g; Fiber: 2g

NOTES

----

98. Cauliflower and Broccoli Cheese Bake

Preparation time: 15 minutes
Cooking time: 35 minutes
Servings: 6

Ingredients:

- One big cauliflower, florets & steamed
- One big broccoli head, florets & steamed
- One tbsp shredded cheddar cheese (ensure it is gluten-free)
- Half cup grated Parmesan cheese (ensure it is gluten-free)
- One & half cups of gluten-free milk
- Three tbsp gluten-free all-purpose flour
- Two tbsp unsalted butter
- Half a tsp ground nutmeg
- Salt & pepper, as required

Directions:

1. Warm up your oven to 375°F.
2. In your medium saucepan, dissolve butter on moderate temp. Add the gluten-free flour and whisk thoroughly, forming a paste.
3. Gradually add the milk while continually whisking, ensuring there are no lumps. Cook this mixture within five mins till it start to thicken.
4. Lower its heat, then mix in half cup cheddar cheese, Parmesan cheese, nutmeg, salt, plus pepper until all cheeses are melted and well combined.
5. In a big baking dish, mix steamed cauliflower and broccoli florets together, spreading them out evenly.
6. Cover the vegetables with the cheese sauce. Sprinkle the remaining half tbsp cheddar cheese on top. Bake within twenty mins till bubbly. Serve.

Nutritional Values (per serving): Calories: 218; Carbs: 19g; Fat: 11g; Protein: 15g; Fiber: 6g

NOTES

----

99. Quinoa Stuffed Butternut Squash

Preparation time: 20 minutes
Cooking time: 40 minutes
Servings: 4

Ingredients:

- One medium butternut squash, halved and seeded
- One cup uncooked quinoa, washed & strained
- Two cups vegetable broth
- One tbsp olive oil
- One small chopped onion
- Two cloves minced garlic
- One cup spinach leaves, chopped
- Half cup cranberries, dried
- Half cup walnuts, chopped
- Salt & pepper, as required

Directions:

1. Warm up your oven to 400°F. Put butternut squash halves on your baking sheet and bake within 30 mins till tender. Cool it down, then scoop out some of the flesh to create a cavity for the stuffing.
2. In your saucepan, let broth boil. Mix in quinoa, cover, then adjust to low temp. Simmer within fifteen mins till all liquid is absorbed. Remove, then let it sit covered before fluffing.
3. In a pan on moderate temp, warm up oil. Put onion and garlic, then cook till onions are soft. Add spinach leaves and cook until wilted.
4. In your big container, combine cooked quinoa, sautéed onion mixture, dried cranberries, walnuts, salt, and pepper.
5. Stuff the cooled butternut squash halves with the quinoa mixture. Return them to the oven, then bake at 350°F within ten mins till heated through. Serve.

Nutritional Values (per serving): Calories 420; Carbs 60g; Fat 18g; Protein 12g; Fiber 10g

NOTES

---

100. Cranberry Orange Glazed Chicken

Preparation time: 15 minutes

Cooking time: 25 minutes

Servings: 4

Ingredients:

- Four no bones & skin chicken breasts
- One cup fresh cranberries
- One orange, zested & juiced
- Half cup gluten-free chicken broth
- Two tbsp honey
- One tbsp olive oil
- Two cloves minced garlic
- Half tsp dried each rosemary & thyme
- Salt & pepper, as required

Directions:

1. Warm up your oven to 375°F.
2. In your medium saucepan, warm up oil on moderate temp. Put garlic, then cook within one min.
3. Add cranberries, zest, orange juice, honey, rosemary, thyme, salt, plus pepper. Let it boil. Adjust to a simmer within ten mins till cranberries have softened.
4. Put chicken breasts in your baking dish, then flavor it using salt and pepper. Pour the cranberry-orange mixture on top.
5. Bake within twenty-five mins till chicken is cooked through. Remove, cool it down, then serve.

Nutritional Values (per serving): *Calories: 301; Carbs: 29g; Fat: 9g; Protein: 28g; Fiber: 2g*

NOTES

CHAPTER 9:
DINING OUT AND
SOCIALIZING

Navigating the world of dining out and attending events can be a challenging experience for individuals with celiac disease or gluten sensitivities. However, being gluten-free should not hold you back from enjoying life's memorable moments and social gatherings. Here are the necessary tools, tips, and strategies to confidently explore restaurants and attend events while maintaining a gluten-free lifestyle.

1. Research Your Options: Before visiting a restaurant or event, take some time to research your options. Utilize resources such as online reviews, gluten-free forums, and smartphone apps designed specifically for locating gluten-free-friendly dining establishments. A well-informed decision will help you to feel more secure in knowing that your chosen location emphasizes gluten-free options and understands the significance of adhering to a strict diet.

2. Communicate Your Needs Clearly: When dining out or attending an event, communication is key. Inform your server or event organizer about your gluten-related concerns and ask for recommendations for suitable menu items. Don't be afraid to inquire about ingredients, preparation methods, and possible cross-contamination risks. Most restaurants are happy to accommodate dietary restrictions when given adequate notice.

3. Learn to Modify Meals: Sometimes you may find that a desired dish at a restaurant contains gluten-based ingredients. In these instances, don't hesitate to request modifications or substitutions. For example, ask for grilled chicken served on lettuce instead of between two slices of bread or opt for rice instead of pasta as a side dish.

4. Carry Gluten-Free Snacks: When attending events where food availability and options may be limited, it's wise to carry some gluten-free snacks with you. Choose portable options like nuts, dried fruit, and protein bars that can tide you over until you can find appropriate meal options.

5. Be Prepared with a Gluten-Free Restaurant Card: A helpful tool during your dining experiences is a gluten-free restaurant card. These cards explain your dietary needs in detail and help chefs, staff, and event organizers to better understand your specific requirements. You can create your own card or download a pre-made version online.

6. Build a Support Network: Establishing a support network is essential for those following a gluten-free lifestyle. Connecting with others who share the same dietary restrictions can provide you with valuable tips, recipes, and restaurant recommendations. Participate in local celiac or gluten-free support groups, attend workshops, and join online forums to expand your knowledge and build relationships.

7. Embrace New Experiences: Don't let fear or uncertainty hold you back from exploring new restaurants and events! As you become more comfortable navigating the gluten-free landscape, you will find that there are plenty of opportunities to enjoy delicious food and meaningful experiences without compromising your health.

Sharing Your Journey: Building a Supportive Gluten-Free Community

Living with celiac disease can be challenging, especially when it comes to maintaining a strict gluten-free diet in a world filled with gluten. However, you're not alone in this journey, and building a supportive community can make your gluten-free lifestyle more enjoyable and sustainable. Let's explore the importance of connecting with others and how you can build a support network to help you thrive as a celiac individual.

1. The Importance of Community: Human beings are social creatures, and we often rely on fellow individuals to help us navigate through life's ups and downs. A supportive gluten-free community can provide empathy, understanding, practical advice, and even introduce you to mouth-watering recipes you haven't tried before! Moreover, being part of such a group will allow you to exchange experiences and learn from everyone's unique insights.

2. Connecting with Others Online: By joining online groups or following social media accounts dedicated to gluten-free or celiac advocacy, you'll have access to a wealth of resources at your fingertips.

Online forums: Websites such as Celiac.com or Gluten Free Society offer platforms where individuals can engage in informative discussions or ask questions related to their lifestyle.

Social media: Platforms like Facebook, Instagram, or Pinterest provide bountiful resources for gluten-free recipes and tips; just search for "gluten-free" or "celiac" hashtags.

Blogs: Many individuals share their journey by writing about their personal experiences or sharing innovative recipes on blogs like Gluten-Free Goddess or Celiac in the City.

3. Creating Local Support Groups: Although online connections are valuable, bonding with others in person can also deeply enrich our lives. Here's how you can establish local support groups:

Leverage social networking platforms: Sites like Meetup.com allow you to create or join existing local groups for individuals with gluten sensitivities or celiac disease. You can participate in various events, ranging from recipe swaps to educational seminars.

Coordinate with nearby medical professionals: Reach out to local gastroenterologists, allergists, or dietitians and inquire about any existing celiac support groups in your region.

Start your own group: If no local support groups are available in your area, why not create one? You can utilize social media to invite potential members and collaborate on planning gatherings.

4. Participating in Awareness Events: Celiac and gluten-free awareness events, such as fundraisers, conferences, or walkathons, provide excellent opportunities for networking and expanding your support network. By attending these events, you'll be able to connect with a broader community of individuals who share your goals and experiences.

5. Spreading the Word: Finally, as part of the gluten-free community, it's crucial to not only engage with fellow members but also spread awareness beyond the celiac circle. Educating friends, family members, and even restaurants about the importance of adhering to a strict gluten-free diet will help foster understanding and create a more inclusive environment.

Sharing your journey as a celiac individual is not only empowering but also beneficial in fostering a supportive community. By connecting with others both online and in-person while participating in awareness-raising events, you'll be able to enhance the quality of your life while living a fulfilling gluten-free journey. Remember that you're not alone in this adventure – together; we can continue to thrive.

CHAPTER 10:
BEYOND THE COOKBOOK

As you embark on your gluten-free culinary journey, it is crucial to stock your pantry with ingredients that are not only free from gluten but also provide a wide range of flavors and textures to make your dishes stand out. Below are the must-have ingredients for any celiac-friendly pantry.

1. Gluten-Free Flour Blends: A good all-purpose gluten-free flour blend can work wonders in your recipes. These blends usually consist of rice flour, tapioca starch, potato starch, and xanthan gum, mimicking the properties of traditional wheat flour. Keep a bag of this essential ingredient on hand to make gluten-free breads, cakes, cookies, and more.

2. Whole Grains and Seeds: Enhance your meals with various gluten-free whole grains like quinoa, brown rice, millet, and teff. Additionally, seeds such as chia, flaxseed, sunflower seeds, and pumpkin seeds add nutritional value and texture to your dishes.

3. Nut Flours: In place of wheat flour, you can use almond flour or coconut flour for those with nut allergies or celiac disease. These flours lend a rich and robust taste to baked goods, providing an extra depth of flavor while supporting a healthy lifestyle.

4. Gluten-Free Pasta: Made from corn, rice or quinoa flour, gluten-free pasta can be found in various shapes like spaghetti or fusilli to help you continue enjoying classic pasta dishes like lasagna or spaghetti Bolognese.

5. Rice: This universally beloved ingredient comes in many flavorful varieties like Basmati or Jasmine which taste great both as side dishes or as the star component in a meal by itself.

6. Gluten-Free Breads: Choose from pre-made loaves or experiment with homemade recipes using gluten-free flours to satisfy cravings for pancakes, sandwiches or French toast.

7. Legumes: Beans, lentils, and peas offer significant amounts of protein and fiber that are essential in a gluten-free diet without sacrificing taste or texture.

8. Fresh Produce: From leafy greens to colorful bell peppers, fresh fruits and vegetables bring life to any dish while providing your body with essential vitamins and minerals.

9. Gluten-Free Condiments: Some condiments may contain gluten, so it's essential to read labels thoroughly. Search for gluten-free soy sauce, mustard, ketchup, and other condiments that will add flavor to your dishes without compromising on safety.

10. Herbs & Spices: Spices like cumin or paprika are naturally gluten-free and can elevate the flavors of your dishes. Keep a variety of herbs on hand to enhance the taste of any meal while keeping things celiac-friendly.

Creating a well-stocked pantry of gluten-free ingredients is key when catering for a celiac diet. It enables you to prepare delicious meals without compromising on taste and reducing the risk of cross-contamination. With these must-have ingredients in your pantry, you'll be well-equipped to whip up tasty recipes from "The Celiac Cookbook" with confidence and ease.

Your Gluten-Free Adventure: Tips for Sustainable Gluten-Free Living

Embarking on a gluten-free adventure can be daunting, yet rewarding for those diagnosed with celiac disease or simply striving to live a healthier lifestyle. Here are some tips and tricks to make your journey sustainable and enjoyable while maintaining a gluten-free diet.

1. Education is Key: Be well-versed in the basics of celiac disease, gluten sensitivity, and gluten-free ingredients. Understanding your condition will help you make informed decisions about your food choices.

2. Become an Expert Label Reader: Learn to scrutinize food labels carefully to identify hidden sources of gluten. Remember that ingredients with names like wheat, barley, rye, malt, and brewer's yeast are off-limits.

3. Plan Your Meals: Pre-planning your meals will save you time and make it easier to stick to a gluten-free regimen. Having a weekly meal plan also helps you monitor and rotate your nutrient intake.

4. Keep Your Kitchen Gluten-Free: Dedicate an area in your kitchen specifically for preparing and storing gluten-free items and cooking utensils. Cross-contamination poses a significant risk for those with celiac disease.

5. Build a Support System: Connect with others who live with similar dietary restrictions to share experiences, recipes, recommendations, and emotional support.

6. Find Your Favorite Gluten-Free Brands: Experiment with different brands of gluten-free products until you find ones that meet your taste preferences, nutritional needs, and budget constraints.

7. Embrace Whole Foods: Incorporate naturally gluten-free whole foods into your diet, such as fruits, vegetables, lean meats, pseudo-grains like quinoa and buckwheat, and nuts/seeds.

8. Dine Out Confidently: When eating out or traveling, research the restaurant options beforehand to identify gluten-free menus or dishes that can be easily modified. Don't hesitate to communicate your dietary requirements to the staff.

9. Get Creative in the Kitchen: Explore gluten-free cooking and baking techniques with various flours, binders and substitutions. You may discover new flavor profiles and create personalized signature dishes.

10. Seek Professional Guidance: Consult a registered dietitian or nutritionist specializing in celiac disease or gluten-free lifestyles for tailored advice to optimize your health.

Making sustainable changes to your lifestyle can be challenging, but by following these tips, you'll be well on your way to thriving on your gluten-free adventure. Each step makes a difference, so stay committed and enjoy the many benefits that come with a gluten-free lifestyle. Happy eating!

CONCLUSION

Celiac disease has left millions of people feeling isolated and overwhelmed, unable to enjoy food without fearing the adverse reactions that gluten can bring. However, this book has set forth to change that notion and provide the necessary tools to transform one's situation into an opportunity for exploration and rediscovery.

The power of food should never be underestimated, especially for those who have been forced to alter their eating habits significantly. This cookbook has brilliantly showcased an array of delicious, gluten-free recipes that prove celiac disease does not always equate to a life devoid of culinary pleasure. By focusing on nourishing ingredients, alternative grains, and creative flavor combinations, readers have learned to craft satisfying meals that cater to their unique dietary needs.

Not only has this book offered go-to recipes for breakfast, main entrees, snacks and dessert, it has also provided essential guidance on managing celiac disease beyond the kitchen. From reading labels and understanding cross-contamination risks to educating oneself about gluten-free products, living with celiac disease can be manageable when properly equipped with practical knowledge.

It is important to acknowledge that adapting to a gluten-free lifestyle is not a linear process - there will be moments of frustration and trial and error. Yet, it is through these challenges that individuals rise above their circumstances and discover newfound resilience and self-awareness.

It is crucial to remember that living with celiac disease or gluten intolerance does not define one's entire existence. Rather than dwelling on past experiences or what could have been, embrace the present moment while savoring each bite from your newly-expanded culinary repertoire. This cookbook is a testament that our health can be both enjoyable and liberating when we allow ourselves the space for creativity and growth.

So, close this book with gratitude in your heart, take it as a valuable companion on your journey, and remember that delicious, comforting, and wholesome gluten-free food is always within reach.

Printed in Great Britain
by Amazon

29322235R00071